A DYBBUK

or Between Two Worlds

A Dramatic Legend in Four Acts

Adaptation by
Tony Kushner

Written by
S. Ansky

Translated from Yiddish by
Joachim Neugroschel

BROADWAY PLAY PUBLISHING INC
224 E 62nd St, NY, NY 10065
www.broadwayplaypub.com
info@broadwayplaypub.com

A DYBBUK OR BETWEEN TWO WORLDS
© Copyright 1998 Tony Kushner

First edition: July 2017
I S B N: 978-0-88145-705-6

Book design: Marie Donovan
Page make-up: Adobe InDesign
Typeface: Palatino

A DYBBUK OR BETWEEN TWO WORLDS received its world premiere in February 1995 at Hartford Stage Company, Hartford, Connecticut.

The play was produced in November 1997 at New York City's Joseph Papp Public Theater/New York Shakespeare Festival.

CAST

CHONEN, a former yeshiva student, now a rabbi, who, having wandered, has returned to Brinnitz

THE THREE BATLONIM, or idlers, who are employed by the community to hang out at the synagogue to fill out a minyan when necessary

THE MESSENGER

MAYER, the shammes (beadle) of the Brinnitz synagogue

OLD WOMAN, named Channa-Esther, whose daughter is dying

HENECH, a yeshiva student, a friend of Chonen

FRADDE, Leah's old nurse

LEAH, the daughter of Sender of Brinnitz

GITL, Leah's friend

SIX OR SEVEN YESHIVA STUDENTS, studying late in the Brinnitz synagogue

SENDER OF BRINNITZ, a wealthy man, follower of Rabbi Azriel of Miropol

TWO OR THREE WEALTHY FRIENDS OF SENDER

FOUR BEGGARS

A POOR WOMAN WITH A BABY

A LAME WOMAN

A VERY HOMELY MAN

A VERY OLD POOR WOMAN

BESSYE, Leah's friend

NACHMAN, father of the bridegroom

RABBI MENDL, teacher of the bridegroom

MENASHE, the bridegroom

MRS. NACHMAN, MENASHE'S AUNTS and UNCLES and COUSINS

A TALL PALE WOMAN

THREE PASSENGERS

RABBI AZRIEL OF MIROPOL, a great Chasidic rabbi, a tzaddik

MICHL, the gabbe (manager) of Rabbi Azriel

THE SCRIBE, Azriel's court's recording secretary

RABBI SHIMSHIN, the Chief Rabbi of Miropol

THREE CHASIDS, all followers of Rabbi Azriel of Miropol

TWO RABBINICAL JUDGES

The first and second acts take place in Brinnitz,
the third and fourth acts take place in Miropol,
in Poland, at the end of the nineteenth century.

Act One

Before the curtain, in near darkness, Chonen is washing himself in a ritual bath. He chants:

CHONEN

Why did the soul,
Oh tell me this,
Tumble from Heaven
To the Great Abyss?
The most profound descents contain
Ascensions to the heights again . . .

(Darkness engulfs the scene.)

The curtain rises slowly.
A small wooden synagogue; its walls blackened with great age and candlesmoke. The roof is held up by two wooden columns. At the center of the ceiling, above the sloping bimah (the platform from which the Torah is read), an old brass lamp, with a single light, is hanging. The bimah is covered with a dark tablecloth. On the rear wall, several small windows with wooden grillwork indicate the womens' gallery. A long table with a wooden bench; on the table are heaps of books, sacred texts, scrolls. Among the books are a few clay candleholders in which tallow candles are burning. To one side of the table, in the rear wall also, is the small door to the rabbi's private study. In a corner near the door is a bookcase containing very old sacred books. In the center of the right-hand wall is the Holy Ark, in which the Torah scrolls are kept. To the left of the Ark is the cantor's rough wooden lectern, upon which a large yahrzeit (memorial) candle is burning, guttering, dripping wax. On either side of the Holy Ark is a window, dark now, it's late at night. There are benches and bookcases along the length of the rest of the wall. On the left-hand wall there is a large tile stove, next to which is another bench and a table, laden with holy books; next to this is a ritual washstand, behind which is a towel hanging from an iron towel ring. Near the washstand is the wide door that leads to the street. Near the door there is a chest; above the chest there is a ner-tomid (an eternal light in a glass-chimneyed hanging lamp). Henech is sitting on a bench near the cantor's stand, studying a holy book. Five or six younger yeshiva students are sprawled on the bench at the rear wall, drowsing through texts while softly humming a dreamy Talmudic melody. Mayer, the beadle, is laying out cloth sacks containing prayer shawls and phylacteries.

The three Batlonim (idlers), heads in the clouds, books face-down on their laps, are sitting at the left-wall table, schmoozing and klatching. The Messenger is lying on the bench near the stove, his head resting on his traveler's pack. In the corner, Chonen stands by the case full of ancient texts, silent and remote, thinking, praying to himself.

Deep evening has settled into the synagogue, deepening its shadowy corners, creating a mysterious, mystical atmosphere.

FIRST BATLON

Before the soul can be inspired,
Holiness is first attired
In glory which the world can see,
In Visible Epiphany!

SECOND BATLON

The Levites, in the days of Old,
Dressed themselves in Cloth of Gold!

FIRST BATLON

And even now, bejeweled, impearled,
Tzaddikim walk the lower world!

SECOND BATLON

Rabbi Dovid of Talna sat on a big chair made all of gold. Rabbi Yisroel of Rizhin of blessed memory went about in a gold-curtained carriage pulled by six gray horses.

THIRD BATLON

Rabbi Shmuel of Kaminka always wore gold slippers. And that's not apocryphal: I personally saw them. Gold slippers!

THE MESSENGER
(Sitting up on the bench, in a quiet, faraway voice) Rabbi Zusye
of Anapol lived and died in poverty. His clothes were
peasants' rags and he begged in the streets. But he was as
holy as anyone who's lived.

*(Little pause. The Batlonim look at the recumbent stranger, who
has not risen from his bench.)*

FIRST BATLON
Pardon me, but who asked you to contribute?

THE MESSENGER
I was intrigued. I have some experience of the wide world,
and I have rarely seen that Holiness attires itself in expensive
clothes.

FIRST BATLON
Of course! But gold is symbolic!

THIRD BATLON
A metaphor! For holiness! Gold in and of itself is valueless,
but . . .

SECOND BATLON
Oh don't jump to that conclusion so hastily! Poor Jews
always equate poverty and virtue, and that's why we stay
poor! We're suspicious of gold. And why? Because when
we dwelt in the Holy Land we were surrounded by mighty
nations of great wealth and sensuality. As the Torah and
the Prophets tell us: the Assyrians had stone cities and
brazen armies, the Babylonians their fragrant gardens, the
Phoenicians their great ports and marketplaces, and the
golden palaces of Pharaoh in Mitzrayim. So in opposition

to these cruel and sensual peoples we developed a violent loathing for the splendor of surfaces. To this day!

FIRST BATLON

Interesting point. Did the Almighty not give us the sun? And moon- and candlelight? And do these bright and flickering lights not radiate from the Holy fire, and doesn't gold magnify and worship the light? Is gold not therefore Holy? It comes from the Almighty! I think it's an interesting point.

THIRD BATLON

It's tricky and dangerous. I fear all such twisty argumentation! This is a shul! A holy place! Think only of holiness here, talk of gold leads to talk of desire which leads to talk of . . . of *women* and talk of women . . . Well, men are from earth and women are from bone, as it's written.

FIRST BATLON

I agree, let's not talk about such things, not here, not at night, we'll inadvertently summon The Evil One. *(He spits)*

SECOND BATLON

(Spitting, then) The Devil can't enter a Holy place, not even if you invoke Him! There's nothing in the Holy books, no chants or incantations, not even in the Kabbalah for calling forth Satan. *(He spits)*

THE MESSENGER

Actually there is a way.

(Chonen looks up and turns toward the Messenger, who directs the following at him:)

THE MESSENGER

Whisper the Unutterable Name of God, once, which is a terrible sin, and then twice. It is after this act of defiance that the Angel of Light was hurled from Paradise into abysmal eternal night. And he waits in night there to answer the call of his acolytes.

THIRD BATLON

It's terribly dangerous to even think of speaking that Name.

THE MESSENGER

For Jews there is always danger everywhere. But the vessel will burst only if the spark within lusts too hotly for the flame without.

FIRST BATLON

In the shtetl of my birth there's a miracle-working rabbi who can make candles ignite by whispering the Holy Name, and if he whispers it again they all go out. He can see for hundreds of miles around, he knows everything that's happening, he drums his fingers on stone walls and wine dribbles from the cracks. He told me he'd made a golem, back when the persecutions grew too frequent and too fierce; he told me how he'd made the dead rise, he could fly invisible through the air and devils danced at his behest. He even conjured Satan. *(He spits)* My rabbi is the one who told me: "Within and within, turn your eyes inwards . . . "

CHONEN

(In a voice like the Messenger's, a faraway voice) Where can I find him?

FIRST BATLON

Who?

CHONEN

This rabbi who works miracles.

FIRST BATLON

He's . . . In his house, I imagine, in my shtetl, if he's still amongst the living.

CHONEN

Is it far?

FIRST BATLON

My shtetl? In deepest Polisia, leagues away. It would take a month at least to walk there.

CHONEN

What's his name?

FIRST BATLON

Why, Reb Chonen? You want to visit him?

(Chonen stares at the Batlonim, and then at the Messenger, silent.)

FIRST BATLON

The shtetl's called Krasne. The rabbi's name is Elchonen.

CHONEN

Thank you.

(He starts to turn back to his corner, but stops and looks at the First Batlon.)

El-Chonen. The God of Chonen. Perhaps I should visit him.

(Chonen goes back to his corner.)

THE MESSENGER
(To the First Batlon) Who is he?

FIRST BATLON
A yeshiva student.

(Mayer closes the gate in front of the bimah and comes over to the table.)

SECOND BATLON
Some sort of genius, they say. A prodigious memory.

THIRD BATLON
He's swallowed over five hundred pages of the Talmud, every letter, every word. The boy's got a magical mind.

THE MESSENGER
Where's he from?

MAYER
A Litvak, I think. He studied here, best of the whole yeshiva, he was elevated to the rabbinate, easy, but then for a whole year following his ordination, he disappeared! Some said he was atoning for sins, others that he wandered in exile; and then, just recently, he came back! But he's not the same boy who left. For one thing, he's a million miles away, all the time, deep inside his thoughts. He doesn't eat anything, except on Shabbes, and then not so much as would satisfy a mouse. And day and night he's in the ritual baths, washing; he's just come from there. *(Lowering his voice)* He's reading the Kabbalah . . .

THIRD BATLON

For instance?

FIRST BATLON

Like in my father's time, even rich from a rich family, when a man sought a suitor for his daughter, he would bring the Grand Rebbe of some Great Yeshiva a nice gift and say, "Which is the best student?" Not who is the richest student, but the smartest, the most wise. Maybe Sender should be doing that.

THE MESSENGER

His daughter's bridegroom might be right here.

THIRD BATLON

Here?

(The Messenger shrugs.)

THIRD BATLON

Marriages are made when the bride and the groom belong to each other. They can't be arranged, not really.

(The outside door bursts open and an Old Woman enters.)

OLD WOMAN

Out of my way, everyone.

MAYER

Woman, go away, you're not permitted here!

OLD WOMAN

I must come in! I want to shove my head in the Ark!

MAYER

God forbid!

OLD WOMAN

I want to shriek at the Torahs. I want to douse the flickering little ner-tomid light with my tears. The King of the Universe is taking my child! MY DAUGHTER IS DYING!

(The students and Batlonim hiss and shush her.)

THIRD BATLON

You see, this is why women aren't permitted in the . . .

OLD WOMAN

God of Abraham, Isaac and Jacob, please don't take my daughter from this world, look at how young she is! Matriarchs, run up to the throne of the Lord of Creation, shout your grief as loudly as I shout mine, tell Him who made you, Matriarchs, on my daughter's behalf, tell Him you will pull the Universe down, stone by stone, unless He promises He'll restore my daughter completely to life!

MAYER

(Crossing to her) Channa-Esther, quiet please, this shrilling in shul is a sin. Maybe I should find ten men for a minyan, we could chant the psalms?

OLD WOMAN

Do it, do it now, why do you need to ask? She's losing her battle with the butcher-angel, praised be He, hurry!

MAYER

Immediately, but we have to give the men something for their trouble. They're poor.

OLD WOMAN
(Rummaging in her pocket) Here, a ruble. Just make sure they say every psalm.

MAYER
A ruble is just a kopek or two per man, Channa-Esther, perhaps . . .

(The Old Woman heads for the door.)

OLD WOMAN
I can't stand here talking to you, I have to visit every synagogue in Brinnitz! MY DAUGHTER IS DYING!

(She leaves in a hurry.)

THE MESSENGER
Earlier today, another woman was here. She too wanted to put her head in the Ark. Her daughter was in labor, and had been for two days, in terrible pain. She wanted the Almighty to let her daughter give birth. One daughter wrestles with death, the other with birth.

THIRD BATLON
So?

THE MESSENGER
Perhaps the soul of the dying daughter is intended for the body of the baby who won't be born. Who would be born, without a soul? Who wants to die, and relinquish the soul? If this sick daughter dies, the laboring daughter will deliver her child. If the sick daughter recovers, the baby will be born dead.

THIRD BATLON
The world is full of mysteries, and people never see them.

FIRST BATLON

(To the drowsing yeshiva students) Wake up! Come to the rabbi's study, we have psalms to chant for the sake of an ailing mother.

MAYER

Everyone who joins in gets a drink of kvass and a buckwheat cake.

(The students, the Batlonim and Mayer go into the study. Soon a mournful recitation of the First Psalm, "Blessed be the man who walks not in the counsel of the ungodly . . . " is heard from within. The Messenger and Chonen are left behind. The Messenger watches Chonen.)

THE MESSENGER

Chonen?

(Chonen turns. He sees that the Ark is open.)

CHONEN

Who opened the Ark? It's nearly midnight . . .

THE MESSENGER

A grieving woman opened it.

CHONEN

A young woman, or old?

THE MESSENGER

Not young.

CHONEN

Not . . . The Torah scrolls are inside like dark men engulfed in shadow, draped in velvet shawls, bent over mysteries. There are nine scrolls here, the number you get when you add up the letters of "Emes," so truth is here, and each of these nine has four wooden spokes, and four times nine is thirty-six, isn't it, which is a number that confronts me everywhere, every day, thirty-six. There's a name. Leah. What number is the letter Lamed?

THE MESSENGER

Thirty.

CHONEN

Exactly. And Aleph is one, and Hey is five. Thirty-six. So it's Leah, obviously, who is waiting for me everywhere, she's hidden in everything, and thrice thirty-six is one hundred and eight, which is the value of Chonen, and three times . . . But also from Leah, Lamed and Hey, one can spell "Not God." Not from God. Leah Not From God.

THE MESSENGER

A terrible thought.

CHONEN

Yes, but I can't stop thinking it, it wants me to think it, it's always there, waiting to be thought, it even gives me a sunless shadow sort of pleasure. Don't tell anyone . . .

THE MESSENGER

I am a messenger, you can trust to my discretion.

CHONEN

You aren't from Brinnitz, but you seem . . .

THE MESSENGER

Familiar, yes, I seem so to most people, but I'm always a stranger. Tell me a tale, Reb Chonen.

CHONEN

There's a man in this town, wealthy and impressive, a great
. . . hoarder of precious things, and he has a daughter, and
she is . . . I've been back a month and I've seen more than
I want to see but I haven't seen her since returning; I fled
from here, from her, from dreams I had in which she
. . . Wherever I've gone, and I have wandered . . . *very*
far, she follows me, in dreams, she begs me to return, and
in me a certainty has grown, and I am certain it's from
God, that she is *mine*, not his, not her father's nor anyone
else's. God wants me to return, to claim her, to say any
prayer, chant any spell in any book to save her from her
father's . . . from his dealings, but God keeps her from
me." He's shut her up inside, one by one I defeat his plans,
I . . . I'm *impressed*, these incantations *work*! The
Almighty speaks sometimes out of the mouths of
salamanders and unclean things, and I'm . . . *astonished*,
but nothing, nothing brings her to me, and . . .

(Henech enters.)

HENECH

Chonen?

(Chonen turns, and the Messenger disappears.)

HENECH

Come sit by me. You stand in the corner, or you wander
the town, dreaming, fantasizing. You have such a mind
for the Law, but you waste your days playing with
numbers, adding and multiplying, you're no better than a
businessman. Let's read the Holy books together.

CHONEN

What Holy books?

HENECH
(Shocked) The Talmud. The Commentaries.

CHONEN
The Talmud is bleak and cold. The Commentaries are barren. Beneath this earth there's another world just like this one, with farms and forests, oceans, deserts, cities, villages, great storms tossing great ships on the seas, terror in the woods, and ceaseless thunder; but in this underworld there's no sky, and no light, only a black ceiling of gravedirt and root-ends, not lightning bolts, no sun. That's the Talmud. Deep and broad and marvelous enough, but earth above and earth below and you can't ever rise up with the Talmud. The Kabbalah . . . is different.

HENECH
You're lost in the tangled words of that book.

CHONEN
Its thorns have caught my soul up, its branches have hurled me toward Heaven, between its covers I've had glimpses of inner rooms, chambers and back alleys in the palaces of God, I have enfolded my suffering heart in the pages of the Kabbalah and my heart has burst into flame there, eyes within eyes have opened wide and seen the edges of the great dark curtain lift.

HENECH
Listen to me, Chonen. We were students together. You frighten me now, you've flown too far, and I don't trust your means of ascent. Read the Talmud, it can lift you to God, but in slow and sure steps, stone by stone. The Talmud guides you along the true path, and it doesn't let you wander. The Kabbalah is all twisting, deviating, writhing. Don't rush to get to Paradise. Remember the four rabbis:

(He begins to intone a Talmudic melody:)

Four rabbis entered Paradise: Azzai, Zoma, Aher, Akiba.
Rabbi ben Azzai looked about and died.
ben Zoma went mad there, returned a mad wraith,
Trampling tender plants, seducing the young,
Aher crossed over to the Other Side.
But Akiba survived it, strong in his faith.

CHONEN

Those rabbis used to scare me, not anymore. Others have followed them to Paradise and come back—the holiest of men, the Baal Shem Tov did it; not everyone who gets there is destroyed.

HENECH

But you aren't the Baal Shem Tov.

CHONEN

I don't claim to be. I have my own path.

HENECH

Instruct me, explain to me.

CHONEN

I can't.

HENECH

Please. I want to know. I yearn to see Paradise, the same as you, I have a soul that seeks the Fire.

(Little pause.)

CHONEN

The tzaddikim walk among us, and these saints have as

their occupation scrubbing sin from human souls, to renew
the soul's perfect original brightness. But evils crowd 'round
every doorway. Clean a soul of seventy sins, polish it bright,
it will come back at once even more spotted. Purify a whole
generation and the next generation appears, unrepentant.
And each generation grows more stiff-necked, and the
tzaddikim grow fewer and weaker, and to us it seems that
evil is withering the world.

HENECH
Then what should we do?

CHONEN
(Quiet and certain) We should not try to banish sin, but to
make sin holy. Like the goldsmith with his delicate ladles,
his small hot flames, his precise and cautious gestures;
the way the farmer carefully, deliberately divides wheat
from chaff; this is how we purify sin, in the crucibles of our
souls, we purify sin and make sin holy.

HENECH
Holy sin is an impossibility.

CHONEN
God made sin.

HENECH
Not true, Chonen, sin is from the Sitra-achra, it belongs to
the Other Side.

CHONEN
And who made the Other Side? The Sitra-achra is God's
Other Side. Satan is another side of God. And so Satan
must be holy.

HENECH

Please, you're confusing me, I can't understand this.
*(Henech buries his face in the book he's been reading. Chonen
stands over him, bends down to him and whispers:)*

CHONEN

Think of the beautiful Song of Songs. What's it doing in
the Bible?

HENECH

Please don't speak to me, Chonen.

CHONEN

(Overlapping) It's full of desire, it's dangerous to read, but
it's there because, precisely because lust and desire are
the most persistent sins, and in the purifying flame of the
Holiest of Holies, even lust and desire have a sound like
this:

Behold, you are fair, my love, you are fair;
Your eyes are like doves,
You are pleasing and fair,
And our bed is made of soft leaves,
And our roof beam is cedar,
And the walls of our house are of cypress.
I am the rose of Sharon,
A lily of the valleys,
Like a lily among thorns is my love among the daughters.
And my beloved is an apple tree among the trees of the
    wood,
Under his shadow I delighted to sit,
And his fruit was sweet to my tongue.
He has brought me to the banquet hall, and his banner is
love.
Oh refresh me with apples, for I am love-sick . . .

(Leah enters the sanctuary. Chonen instantly stops reciting and stares at her.
Mayer emerges from the rabbi's study, just as, behind Leah, Fradde and Gitl enter. The women hesitate by the door.)

FRADDE
We knocked. Someone was praying and didn't hear us, but we knocked.

MAYER
Sender's daughter! An honor!

LEAH
(Timid) You promised me, Mayer, you'd show me the old curtains for the Ark.

(Leah looks at Chonen, then looks down and doesn't look back.)

FRADDE
You know the ones, Mayer, the old embroidered curtains, Leah promised new ones on the anniversary of her mother's death. She can embroider like they used to, with heavy gold and silver thread, lions and eagles and pomegranates. You can hang the new curtains on the Ark and they'll sparkle like her mother's soul in Paradise.

MAYER
Right away! *(He goes back into the study)*

GITL
(Whispering to Leah) I don't like it here at night, it's grim and frightening.

LEAH
I've never been in a synagogue this late before, except on Simchas Torah, when everyone's dancing and all the

candles are lit. It's brooding tonight, mourning over lost lives, it's heartbreaking, it's dark as the bottom of the sea.

FRADDE

Sure it's a sad place at night and I'll tell you why that is. The dead come to pray here at the shul at night, scattering their sorrows on the floor like dead leaves, leaving piles of sorrows all over the place.

GITL

Stop it, Fradde, you know I hate ghost stories.

FRADDE

And you want to know why the walls are wet? Touch them, see if I'm telling stories—they're wet! That's because every morning when the sun rises fresh on the happy world, the Almighty weeps to remember how the Temple was destroyed, and the walls of every synagogue run wet with His tears. That's why the walls are never cleaned—so we remember how dark and bitter it's been. Whitewash those walls, and stones will fall on your head and kill you.

LEAH

From the outside, or from the balcony, or when it's all lit up, you can't tell how old it is. But it's very very old.

FRADDE

Oh my darling, it's inconceivably old. They say it wasn't built, just found buried underground, the whole building. And even though the village has been burned to the ground again and again, so many times, the synagogue never burns. Once they set the roof afire, but doves came flying, hundreds of doves, from out of the synagogue roof, clasping the flames in their wings, bearing the fire up away from the shul, and so it was saved.

LEAH

I'd like to stay here all night if I could, and kneel by the walls and ask them their secrets, why they weep and for whom, every person, name by name, ask them to tell me what they dream at night. Their silence draws me.

(Mayer returns with the curtains.)

MAYER

Handle them carefully, they're hundreds of years old, they were stitched by a rebbetzin who lived and died among the Jews of Spain, before the exile from there began.

(As they examine the curtains:)

GITL

Leah, there's a boy over there, staring . . .

LEAH

He's from the yeshiva. Chonen.

GITL

You know him?

FRADDE

Look at this velvet. Sure it's disintegrating but how deep the plush is, it's so heavy.

LEAH

Sometimes he came to our house for meals.

GITL

He's afraid of you. He wants to come closer but he can't.

LEAH

He looks pale and thin and unhappy. Do you think he's
been ill?

GITL

Oh I don't think he's unhappy. Look at his eyes.

LEAH

They're always like that, incredible eyes, and when he
talked to me he spoke with short, tight breaths. And that's
how I talked to him.

GITL

No wonder you made Fradde bring us here, it wasn't the
curtains.

LEAH

It's wrong to talk and he's a stranger.

FRADDE

Mayer, we have to go now and we can't visit God without
kissing the Torahs.

MAYER

Naturally, just don't tell the rabbi, let me get one.

*(Mayer goes to the Ark, followed by Gitl and Fradde. Leah lags
behind, and looks at Chonen. A little pause, then:)*

LEAH

Good evening, Chonen. You've come back from your
travels.

CHONEN

(Breathless) Yes. I've . . . returned.

(They look at each other.)

LEAH

You've returned . . .

FRADDE

Leah, come and kiss the Torah!

(Leah goes to Mayer, who's holding the Torah. She kneels, embraces it, and kisses it passionately for a long time.)

FRADDE

That's enough, that's enough, you kiss the Torah quickly, it's made of fire, black and white fire and it'll burn you if you linger. We should get home before your father finds out. *(Nodding goodnight)* Mayer.

(The women leave. Mayer returns the scroll to the Ark and shuts the Ark doors, and then follows the women out.)

CHONEN

(A pause, then)

. . . For I am lovesick . . .
The winter is past, the rain is over and gone,
The time of singing is come,
And the voice of the turtle is heard in our land . . .
Until the days breathe, and the shadows flee away . . .

HENECH

Stop reciting, Chonen.

(Henech strokes Chonen's hair, pulling one of his payes.)

HENECH

Your hair's wet again. You've been to the ritual baths.

CHONEN

Yes.

HENECH

While you're cleansing your body do you chant spells? Is this what's prescribed in the Book of Raziel the Angel?

(Silence, Chonen doesn't respond.)

HENECH

I'd be afraid.

(Little pause.)

You can't live without eating and you never eat now, only on Shabbes and that's not enough.

CHONEN

I want to stop eating on Shabbes. I've grown to hate the smell of food.

HENECH

What in the name of the Almighty are you doing to yourself?

CHONEN

I've seen . . . A diamond, perfect, a perfect thing, absolute, hard and . . . I want to hold her, and cry, until my tears melt the diamond and then . . . I'll drink her in, and then . . . see .
. . something, maybe . . . sunlight striking the domes of the Temple, not the ruined First nor the burnt Second Temple but the Third Temple, the one the future waits to build, I want to see such beauty . . .
(He pauses and sways a little) I am a little weakened by . . . the studies, but . . . There's a way to make gold, did you know

that? Two barrels of gold, by shaping letters in clay, and I need to learn this, to make gold coins for the man whose only love is counting.

HENECH

You can't do work like that through the Holy One.

CHONEN

Then through some Other way.

HENECH

I'm afraid of you, Chonen. Standing beside you, the things you say.

(Henech leaves the sanctuary. Chonen stands alone, motionless. The Batlonim emerge from the rabbi's room.)

FIRST BATLON

Eighteen psalms is psalms enough.

SECOND BATLON

Eighteen after all symbolizes life, and for a few kopeks I'm not going to do all one hundred and fifty psalms.

THIRD BATLON

We should have stayed with the others, we broke the minyan.

SECOND BATLON

They'll be here all night.

(Mayer comes in from the outside.)

MAYER

Well you were right. I just met Borech the tailor coming

home from Klimovke, and he traveled with a man from there who knew the parents of this latest prospect for Sender's daughter, and this man told Borech that Sender and the bridegroom's parents hadn't been able to settle terms, Sender wanting the bridegroom's family to house the couple for ten years, they countered with five years, Sender says it's not enough and so another wedding scratched. Number four!

CHONEN
(*Sitting heavily on a bench, to himself*) I win again.

THIRD BATLON
Four in a row. A real shame.

THE MESSENGER
(*To the Third Batlon*) You said so yourself: the Almighty, not fathers, makes marriages.

THIRD BATLON
Did I say that?

THE MESSENGER
You did.

(*The Messenger stands up, lights his lantern and picks up his pack.*)

THE MESSENGER
Good night everyone. I've stayed longer than I should.

THIRD BATLON
Don't go, let's talk some more.

THE MESSENGER
I'm a messenger, I work for wealthy and powerful clients,

they use me to deliver important messages and convey valuable possessions back and forth. My time is not my own.

MAYER

Stay till dawn at least.

THE MESSENGER

I can't; it takes from midnight to morning to get where I'm going.

THIRD BATLON

That's how long a prayer takes to reach the Throne of Heaven!

THE MESSENGER

I'll be expected at dawn.

(The rest of the minyan emerges from the study.)

A YESHIVA STUDENT

Finished.

THIRD BATLON

That was fast.

SECOND BATLON

Mazel tov.

FIRST BATLON

God grant the poor woman a complete recovery. Let's pool our rubles for some liquor; the night's gotten chilly, my back is stiff.

MAYER

In the house of God you need only ask.

(Mayer produces a bottle of kvass.
Suddenly the front door is flung open and Sender enters, his hat
pushed back, his coat unbuttoned, grinning from ear to ear. Three
or four other men, well dressed, follow him.)

MAYER

Reb Sender! Welcome!

SENDER

I was headed home but I stopped by to check up on you.

(Sender takes the bottle from Mayer, looks at the label.)

SENDER

I knew I'd find you with your noses deep in books. Pious
Chasids every one.

MAYER

Your daughter was here! Moments ago!

SENDER

Leah? Why was she . . .

MAYER

With a bevy of women! Scrutinizing needlework!

FIRST BATLON

We've been overrun with women tonight.

THIRD BATLON

Drink with us, Reb Sender.

SENDER

Oh but absolutely, only we won't need this potato vodka,
I'm buying and it'll be real champagne! Congratulate me! I

have signed the contract for my daughter's marriage!

EVERYONE

Mazel tov! Mazel tov!

(While everyone moves to shake Sender's hand, Chonen stands and retreats to his corner.)

MAYER

The tailor said he'd heard you couldn't arrive at satisfactory terms with the boy's father.

THIRD BATLON

To be honest, our hearts were broken.

SENDER

The tailor didn't hear wrong, but I know how to negotiate, and the boy's father knows how to bend, and so Leah will soon be married!

THE MESSENGER

Chonen, you should leave this corner, join the others.

CHONEN

(To the Messenger) No, this is wrong, it's not what's supposed to be, I've worked so hard, fasted and cleansed myself, I said the terrible Angel's prayers!
(Shouts to heaven) I was promised! I've taken steps down roadways no one's ever walked before, to find her again and . . . and I've been weakened by all these struggles, I can't journey again, I have nowhere else to look, it's . . . I can pronounce the Name—twice. As you said. I can call on God's other angels, the fallen ones, they'll assist me. You are their messenger, this message you brought was intended for me.

THE MESSENGER
I'm only resting here, Chonen. What must be will be.

(*Chonen pulls the Messenger close, and whispers the Name in his ear. The Messenger grimaces in pain. Chonen whispers the Name again, and again the Messenger grimaces.*)

CHONEN
I've finally won, I had to win, she is light and I am flame and wherever she is I will be rekindled . . .

(*Chonen falls to the floor.*)

THE MESSENGER
(*Looking at his lantern*) The candle's guttered out. I'll light a new one.

(*All the lights in the synagogue die out.*)

SENDER
Mayer! What's wrong with the candles? Lights!

THE MESSENGER
Reb Sender?

SENDER
Who is that? What happened to the candles?

THE MESSENGER
You've made a deal with someone?

SENDER
Yes, I . . . MAYER! Candles!

THE MESSENGER

At times it happens that fathers make deals and then later break their promises. And it all winds up in Rabbinical Court.

(Mayer lights a candle.)

THE MESSENGER

So be very careful, Reb Sender.

(Sender goes over to Mayer.)

SENDER

Who's that stranger?

MAYER

Just a messenger, from elsewhere . . .

SENDER

Tell him to leave me in peace. Osher! Run to my house and tell the servants to get a midnight feast ready, like Belshazzar!

(One of the students rushes out.)

SENDER

Let's go to my house, everyone. We'll tell stories along the way, of our Rabbi of Miropol—suddenly I'm all nerves, I don't know why! Who knows a story for the journey?

THE MESSENGER

I do.

SENDER

Perhaps someone else can . . .

THE MESSENGER

The Rabbi of Miropol was visited by a very rich Chasid, who was zealous in some respects but also tight-fisted, a miser. The rabbi took the miser's hand and brought him to a window. "Have a look!" said the rabbi. The miser looked. The rabbi asked, "Well?" The miser said, "I see people on the street." Then the rabbi took his hand again and brought the miser to the hallway mirror. Again the rabbi asked, "Well?" Of course the miser said, "I see myself, Rabbi." The rabbi said, "And do you understand?" Of course the miser didn't. The rabbi said, "The window's made of glass, and so is the mirror. But the mirror has a thin silver coating. All it takes is a silver coat, and suddenly you can't see other people, only yourself."

SENDER

I think you're mocking me.

THIRD BATLON

I liked the story, the rabbi's gentleness is always impressive.

SECOND BATLON

Sing something!

FIRST BATLON

I know a song by the Maggid of Koznitz, who was always infirm but very Holy: it was said in his life he learned this song from the angels, but after his death his disciples informed us: the angels learned it from the Maggid of Koznitz, in fact, these angels who sang were born from his goodness.

(The First Batlon begins to sing a beautiful Chasidic melody; the others join in; the tempo increases.)

SENDER

Let's dance a rikudl! We are Chasids, after all, it's a shame
on my honor if I announce my daughter's engagement,
and no one joins me in a dance. Let us dance because the
Almighty overcomes obstacles and small scrupling and
insists on joy! Please, please, everyone join in!

(They form a circle and begin to dance.)

SECOND BATLON

Where's Henech, and Chonen?

SENDER

Chonen! Yes, Chonen, I forgot about him, come, boy, join
the dancing!

THE MESSENGER

He's over there.

MAYER

(Looking about, seeing Chonen) He's on the floor, exhausted,
asleep.

SENDER

No sleeping tonight, wake him up!

(Mayer tries to wake Chonen, shaking him.)

MAYER

He won't wake up.

*(The others gather around Chonen and try to wake him. When
they realize what has happened:)*

FIRST BATLON

May the Almighty have mercy.

SECOND BATLON

He's dead.

THE MESSENGER

Look at the book in his hand.

THIRD BATLON

From the Kabbalah.

THE MESSENGER

He is destroyed.

Act Two

Three months later. Leah's wedding day. Leah and Fradde in a mikvah. Fradde is holding a sheet while Leah washes herself, preparing for her wedding day.

FRADDE

Now there are three sins for which a woman might die in childbirth, and these are: Not keeping separation when we are bleeding. Not keeping separation for the offering of the first dough. And last, for failing to light the Shabbes candles as a separate blessing. Because in the Talmud it says: "The soul which I have given you is called a candle, and therefore I've given you a commandment concerning candles. If you keep these commandments, well and good—"

LEAH

"—But if not I will take away your soul."

FRADDE

The world is a troubled and mysterious place, don't you think? I think it is a troubled and mysterious place. Well certainly mysterious. And troubled too. I remember a niggun they say was first sung by the wife of the Great Maggid:

(Sings:)

Far away, at one end of the world, the world atop a
mountain,
Pouring from a fissure in a stone, a stone, issues a fountain.
At the other ending of the world, the heart of the world is
     found;
The heart adores the fountain, and longs to drink its waters.
If it ever traveled to the spring, the heart of the world
     would die.
The heart must never travel; but watch and long forever.

Forever, never, never to be there!
Never! Never! To breathe your mountain air!
And never drink you in!
Never plunge within!
Ah, thirsty, longing, burning,
The heart forever watching!

Every living thing requires time: in time the spring is
     living.
Since the spring has no time of its own, its own, the heart
     is giving
To the spring each day a little time, but when the night
     draws nigh,
The spring, afraid of dying, sings to the heart for mercy.
As the heart sings longing in return, another day is made.
Across the world they're calling, with songs of love and
     mercy.

Oh mercy, mercy, give me one more day!
Minutes, hours, let my waters play!
Oh heart of precious time,
Hear your fountain chime
And grant another morning,
Oh heart forever watching.

As their singing spreads across the world, the world, in
 threads of fire,
Shining threads connecting living hearts, the hearts feel
 deep desire.
Every living creature has a heart, and every heart a thread.
And He of Holy Wisdom draws all the threads together.
From the fiery threads is woven time, and thus new days
 are made;
Unto the heart is given, unto the spring is given.
As the spring pours waters through the days, the heart of
 the world looks on.
And so the world continues, until the world is gone.

The wife of the Great Maggid sang this song the night she
conceived Abraham her son, later called Abraham the
Angel, because he was so Holy he wasn't a man. When he
grew up, Abraham the Angel was too awesome to even
look upon, not even his wife could look at him. On their
wedding night Abraham the Angel's wife fainted dead
away when he came to their bed. But she bore him two
sons when she found her courage.
But after that Abraham the Angel lived alone. And so did
his wife.

SCENE 2

Three months later, a square in Brinnitz. To the left is the synagogue, its exterior revealing its antiquity in both style and wear. In front of the synagogue, slightly off to one side, is a mound of earth atop which a very old gravestone is inscribed: "HERE LIE THE PURE AND HOLY BRIDE AND BRIDEGROOM, MARTYRED IN THE YEAR 5408 (1648). BLESSED BE THEIR SOULS." To the right is Sender's handsome wooden home, with a gate, a courtyard that stretches around the front and along the side of the house, and a porch. Behind these buildings the alleys and houses, taverns and shops of Brinnitz stretch away to the riverbank. A windmill is visible, as is the brick bathhouse, the poorhouse, and on the other side of the river, dense dark forests.

On a bluff above the river is the Jewish cemetery with many tombstones.

The gates to Sender's house are open. Long tables extend across his courtyard into the town square. At the tables the town's poor population, beggars and cripples, are eating ravenously. Waiters bring heaping platters of food and baskets of bread from Sender's house.

The people of Brinnitz move about the square, the men going in and out of the synagogue with shawls and phylacteries on, the women in and out of Sender's house with food and gifts. Dance music and the sounds of a crowd are heard from the courtyard behind Sender's house.

It's early evening. The Messenger, wearing an elegant long satin frock coat, his hands tucked behind his back in his belt, is examining the grave of the martyred bride and bridegroom, talking to the First and Third Batlonim.

FIRST BEGGAR
A groschen, a kopek, a shekel, a ruble?

SECOND BEGGAR
Give to the poor, you can afford it!

THIRD BEGGAR
It's a special mitzvah, to give money at a wedding.

FOURTH BEGGAR
Make the beggar-angels happy, give me a ruble.

THE MESSENGER
God forbid us we should be talking about graves at a wedding, but it's an unusual thing, isn't it, a grave in the foreyard of a synagogue.

FIRST BATLON
It's from long ago. There were dreadful pogroms here. The cossack chief Chmielnitski, may he burn forever in Hell, even on Shabbes may he burn.

THIRD BATLON
Amen.

THE MESSENGER
"HERE LIE THE PURE AND HOLY BRIDE AND BRIDEGROOM, MARTYRED IN THE YEAR 5408. BLESSED BE THEIR SOULS."

THIRD BATLON
Well, Amen again.

FIRST BATLON
The cossacks attacked Brinnitz on Easter Sunday, they slaughtered every other person in their path. Hundreds

died, including this bride and her bridegroom, just as they were stepping under the chuppah, and the orchestra was playing. After it was over the pair was buried, husband and wife in a single grave, to mingle dust and bones till Moshiach comes, and ever since then the site is holy. Whenever he performs a marriage, our rabbi hears sighs that come from the earth. And people say sometimes a ghostly orchestra is playing. So in Brinnitz we have a custom: after any wedding, the guests dance around the grave, to cheer up the grieving, martyred dead.

THE MESSENGER
I approve of the custom.

(Mayer enters from Sender's yard.)

MAYER
Have you seen such a party as the party he's throwing?

THE MESSENGER
The dead should not be excluded from any celebration.

MAYER
Sholem aleichem! Back in town! More messages to deliver?

THE MESSENGER
I go where they send me.

MAYER
Well you've timed your visit nicely. Here we are having the wedding to end all weddings!

THE MESSENGER
Even in Paradise they're talking about it.

MAYER

(*Laughing*) Sender thinks he can feed every beggar in Brinnitz! You came by the river road. Did you pass the bridegroom's family on your way?

THE MESSENGER

He'll be here shortly.

MAYER

That's good! They're late!

THE MESSENGER

The bridegroom cometh! He'll be on time.

MAYER

Quick, into the house, have delicious food. Sender, I remember, didn't like you but today, even you will be welcomed! A quarter of a buffle fish and a hunk of roast on every plate, big bowls of carrot soup, and there's cake and honey and real brandy besides. Who knew even Sender had this kind of money?

FIRST BATLON

Sender plays it safe. You have to when you invite the poor to table. Rich guests you know who they are, but a poor guest could be an itinerant tzaddik fond of disguises: the holy ones like to catch the wealthy unawares in the act of being greedy—one of God's thirty-six Just men, one of the lamed vovniks could be in Sender's yard right now!

MAYER

Or even the Prophet Elijah returned could be back there, sitting on a bench, blowing to cool down a spoonful of carrot soup. Didn't Moshiach Himself squat for years

outside the gates of Babylon, disguised as a beggar? And
He never revealed Himself only because no one thought to
ask Him if he was Moshiach, because why would the King
of the World sit among lepers, and then He went away,
unnoticed and unasked-for, back to Heaven, and look at
the trouble we've had ever since. So you have to watch it
with the poor.

THE MESSENGER

Not only the poor. All people are entitled to respect, and
generosity. We've all had lives before this one, and no one
is simply or entirely who he or she appears to be.

*(Mayer leads the Messenger and the First and Third Batlonim
into Sender's house, as Leah, wearing her wedding dress, dances
on from the rear courtyard, her partner a poor woman carrying a
baby. Many other poor women, some old, some on crutches, follow
closely behind, clamoring for a turn with the bride.)*

A POOR WOMAN WITH A BABY

I danced with the bride! And so did the baby!

A LAME WOMAN

I danced with her too, she has such cold fingers!

A VERY HOMELY MAN

I hate this custom, why should only the women dance with
the bride, I could make her spin for real, cold fingers or
cold feet, I know ways to make a bride spin!

(Fradde enters onto Sender's porch.)

FRADDE

Leah, stop dancing with the paupers now, darling, they'll
make you dizzy! Gitl! Bessye!

(Gitl and Bessye enter from inside the house.)

FRADDE
Go rescue Leah, she's being danced to death.

A VERY OLD POOR WOMAN
Not yet, not yet, I haven't had my turn.

A POOR WOMAN WITH A BABY
And Yachne so old she's danced with every bride since
Eve!

A VERY OLD POOR WOMAN
That's enough, you korva, you pinska, snake-eyes . . .

*(Mayer returns from the house with a chair, and he sits in the
square, mopping his brow.)*

MAYER
(Singing:)

Rich papa Sender, avoiding a sin,
Asks beggars and bridegrooms and messengers in!
With rubles and groschen and kopeks in store
For every poor soul who can squeeze through his door!

Sender's got money, a crown for his head,
Rents homes to the living and graves to the dead,
Sells vodka to cossacks, lends gold to the czar,
Knows just who his friends and his enemies are:
His friends are his debtors, all shabby and slim,
And his enemies: those who lend money to him!

THE POOR
(Joining Mayer, singing:)

Zlotys turn rubles when they cross his palms

And the angels in paradise offer him psalms—
Collateral payment when begging for loans.
And even Ha-Shem, on His seven gold thrones,
It's whispered is now one of Reb Sender's debtors;
Ha-Shem has been forced to pawn several letters:
Bet, gimel, dalet, chey, yud and tet!
If the Holy One borrows, who isn't in debt?
We all are, and someday Reb Sender will own
All Brinnitz, the earth, and the Almighty's Throne!

MAYER

Rich papa Sender, obeying the Law
Pries open his purse dropping coins from his craw,
Which leaves his craw free so he's able to pray
For blessings for Leah on her Wedding Day!

(There is a mad dash and much commotion, all the poor fighting their way into Sender's house. Only Gitl, Bessye, Leah, Fradde and the Very Old Poor Woman are left outside. The Very Old Poor Woman grabs Leah and begins to dance with her.)

A VERY OLD POOR WOMAN

I need no food or money now, I'm too old to eat or buy things, only dancing's what I want now, dancing like I used to do, wild wedding dancing 'round the square and 'round the square, till the houses spin and the shops spin and the carts and the horses and the goats spin up and the synagogue whirls like a top and all of Brinnitz lifts, up, up, into the woozy yellow sky, and the river's in the air and the cobblestones float like clouds, and I am as young as you are Leah, and you're even older than me!

(Gitl intervenes, stopping the dancing pair. Gitl pries the old woman away.)

A VERY OLD POOR WOMAN
No! More, please! More please! Not yet, don't take me yet!
(Bessye supports Leah as Gitl leads the old woman away.)

FRADDE
Leah, you're bone-white and worn out, come sit on the porch.

LEAH
I'm fine, I'm fine.

BESSYE
They've dirtied your gown! It's spoiled!

GITL
Let's get rags and wipe it clean before . . .

LEAH
(In a faraway voice) Don't leave me alone, if you leave a bride alone unmarried, the envious ones on the Other Side . . . *(She laughs)*

FRADDE
Leah, are you out of your mind, darling, don't talk about evil things on your wedding day! Spit!
(Fradde, Bessye and Gitl spit.)

FRADDE
Twice more!

(Fradde, Bessye and Gitl spit twice more.)

LEAH
My mouth's gone dry, they danced the spit out of me, their need was so overwhelming everything flowed out of me, warmth and wetness, I dried, I felt airborne like an old

tamarind husk on the wind . . .

FRADDE

Leah, darling . . .

LEAH

The souls of the Other Side are everywhere, Fradde, and
your spitting doesn't worry them, because they aren't
evil, only dead, cut down while still young, and there
are so many of them, so many everywhere, bodies buried
everywhere, souls of the dead in the air . . .

FRADDE

Souls of the righteous rest in the bright lights of Paradise,
Leahlah, they're up on high, not here in Brinnitz, which is
only for the living, and those who don't belong.

(Fradde spits.
The Messenger enters and stands unobtrusively apart.)

FRADDE

Now come inside, rest yourself, eat something warm . . .

LEAH

What about the ones who have been cheated of long lives,
what about the ones who die too soon? What becomes of
everything they were supposed to do, the tears unshed,
the happy days never spent in happiness? The children they
never had together, all of that, does all that unspent life have
no place to go? Once upon a time there was a boy with a
great mind and a soul as tall as the towers of Jerusalem,
oh he was beautiful and he would have been beautiful for
ninety years more, but he died while he was still a boy, in
an instant he was dead. They put him in the ground, in
earth that wasn't ready to receive him, with prayers on his
lips he never had time to pray, and words for people he

didn't have the breath to speak. Fradde, blow a candle out and if it's still tall and straight you simply light it again, you don't throw it out; if a life is extinguished before its vessel has grown frail and broken, it can't be forever, its flame can be rekindled.

FRADDE

Leah, my only darling, it's your wedding day and you shouldn't be thinking about anyone but the bridegroom, and nothing unhappy, and God forbid nothing unholy, for only Alvinu Malchenu knows why anything is.

LEAH

My mother died young. She didn't even have time to know why she was put here on earth, and then she was taken. Fradde, I want to go to the cemetery now and invite mother to come to my wedding, to wait with my father by the chuppah and lead the marital procession, and then dance with me like we did when I was very small. I've seen her, Fradde, on the Holy Days, on the Festivals, at Pesach she watches us from the cold without, hoping to be asked in . . . The dead will talk to you if you permit them; this martyred couple, the holy bride and bridegroom, they visit me night after night, and they were young and terribly beautiful and each was bursting with joy when they stepped under the canopy, and the music was so joyful it hid the clatter of horses' hooves, and the scent from the baking ovens was so sweet it masked the devil's stench, and the first stroke of the axe scattered his teeth across the square, and the horses' hooves tore through her dress as she ran, and they seized her veil with their hands and . . .

GITL

Leah, stop! It's horrible!

FRADDE

Leah, come in and lie down till your bridegroom arrives—
where do you suppose he could . . .

LEAH

Holy bride and bridegroom! I invite you to my wedding!
Come stand with me under the canopy, stand close so I can
feel you near me . . .

*(There is a sudden blast of wedding music from a klezmer orchestra.
All four women scream, and Leah nearly faints.)*

GITL

It's alright, it's alright, it's the bridegroom finally arrived!
Leah, we'll go see what he's like.

FRADDE

You're supposed to tell her only one thing: black hair or
blond!

BESSYE

Is it alright, Leah?

(Leah nods yes.)

GITL

Come on!

(Gitl and Bessye run off. The Messenger approaches Leah.)

THE MESSENGER

Bride.

LEAH

What . . . ? *(Leah stares at him)* What do you want?

THE MESSENGER

Let me tell you something; I speak with a certain authority. The souls of the dead are everywhere, as you say, but souls always seek bodies, because only through the flesh can a soul purify itself. Some souls must pass through a number of bodies before they are cleansed.

Sinful souls, bride, enter the bodies of beasts of the ground, birds of the air, even plants, and there, unable to achieve holiness, they await a tzaddik, who sees their plight, and sets them free. Some souls enter the bodies of infants, and by doing good in their new lives they ascend.

LEAH

I understand.

THE MESSENGER

And then there are souls, troubled and dark, without a home or resting place, and these attempt to enter the body of another person, and even these are trying to ascend.

(Sender calls from inside his house.)

SENDER

Leah, come, the bridegroom's finally arrived!

THE MESSENGER

And such a soul is called a dybbuk.

(The Messenger vanishes. Leah doesn't move. Sender enters.)

SENDER

Leah!

FRADDE

She's catching her breath, she danced with the poor and they wore her out, let her rest her nerves, she's nervous.

SENDER

It's a mitzvah to dance with the poor and to feed them. *(He looks at the sky)* The sky's already dark, we have to start soon.

FRADDE

She hasn't gone to the graveyard yet.

(Sender goes to Leah.)

SENDER

Go to your mother, my darling daughter, we'll wait, tell her Sender is waiting for her, to hold her hand at her daughter's wedding. Let her see the fine Jewish woman I raised up in you, and bid her to come meet your husband, who is a student, and respectful, and from a very good family with marvelous connections.

(Sender wipes his tears away, kisses Leah and returns to the house.)

LEAH

There's someone else in the graveyard Fradde, and I want to invite him too.

FRADDE

You ask only Mother and your grandpa and your aunt Mirele may they shine in Paradise. The dead are lonely and if you start asking other than family, the ones who don't get asked get jealous and angry.

LEAH

Just one other.

FRADDE

Really Leah I'm scared to do that. You know the talk, they
say he died in uncleanliness, in horrible sin, his grave isn't
even marked. Nobody knows where it is.

LEAH

I know where he's buried. He's told me where.

FRADDE

God protect us.

LEAH

He asked that I invite him tonight.

(Gitl and Bessye enter.)

BESSYE

He's here!

GITL

I saw him!

BESSYE

Blond hair!

GITL

No, jet black!

BESSYE

Blond!

GITL

Let's go look again.

(They exit.
Leah starts to leave in the opposite direction.)

FRADDE

Leah, wait for Fradde, next you'll be wanting to go there alone, such a strange girl . . .

(They exit. The stage is momentarily empty, and gloomy.
Music, and then Nachman, father of the bridegroom; Rabbi Mendl,
the bridegroom's teacher; and Menashe, the bridegroom, tiny,
pigeon-chested, pop-eyes like a newt's. The bridegroom's family—
his mother, aunts, uncles and cousins follow after. Sender comes
out of the house to greet them.)

SENDER

Sholem aleichem Reb Nachman and family! Welcome, Menashe, Rabbi Mendl, Mrs. Nachman, everyone welcome!

(Kisses and handshakes all around.)

SENDER

Reb Nachman my friend you're terribly late! We worried.

NACHMAN

You wouldn't believe this trip! We were on the river road but it seems to have doubled in length and forked many times since I was last on it, which was only last month. And the roadbed has fallen into disrepair, at one point it just vanishes into a great marsh that wasn't there before, we were almost stuck for the night. My wife says that demons, God should protect us, were trying to keep us out of Brinnitz.

MRS. NACHMAN

Demons! Pooh pooh pooh!

NACHMAN

But I have a seasoned and determined team of mules, mules with fire in their nostrils and with demon-defying spirits.

SENDER

Perhaps you need to rest a bit, before . . .

MRS. NACHMAN

Oh no, there's too much to tie up, the dowry contract, the distribution of gifts, the rabbi's fees, the cantor and the beadle and the orchestra. The fathers must talk!
(The two fathers walk up and down the square, transacting.)

RABBI MENDL

(To Menashe) Menashe, remember, during the meal you're to sit quietly at the table, don't fidget, don't squirm, eat the food, don't leave and wander off, or I'll kill you. And keep your eyes down, you're supposed to, don't bug about the room the way you do. As soon as they've cleared the dishes the shammes gets up and says: "The bridegroom will commence his Talmudic exegesis," and you are to recite the whole story letter-perfect . . .

MENASHE

"Holy Rabbi Meir had a wise wife named Beruria, and she had a light-headed sister who . . . "

RABBI MENDL

Yes, exactly, not now, after they take the plates away, stand on your chair, sing out in a manly voice, the louder the better, and remember, letter-perfect, or I'll kill you. Don't be frightened. MENASHE! You hear me?!?

MENASHE

Rabbi. I *am* frightened.

RABBI MENDL

Of what? You know everything, I taught you, did you forget your Talmudic exegesis?

MENASHE

I remember, but . . .

RABBI MENDL

But what?

MENASHE

The journey here was so scary. And everyone's *staring* at me like I'm a gypsy's monkey. I hate the eyes of strange people, I hate being stared at.

RABBI MENDL

That's your Aunt Rochele's evil eye at work, but I gave you an amulet . . .

MENASHE

And mostly Rebbe I am afraid of her! That girl! I've had dreams, she's terrifying, I shouldn't have come here, I want to hide in a burrow in the ground, Rebbe, I . . . *(He sees the grave of the Holy Couple) Rebbe! It's a grave!* What sort of people put a grave in their town square? I don't want to be married Rebbe, when we thank God in the morning he didn't make us women, no one's more grateful than I am, Rebbe, I don't want to get married, I'm ugly, she has terrible burning eyes, I don't . . .

RABBI MENDL

Menashe! You're to stop this immediately! Or you'll forget your speech and you'll make me look stupid! Come, let's rehearse.

(*A Tall Pale Woman, A Very Old Poor Woman, A Poor Woman with a Baby, A Very Homely Man and the other poor people enter from Sender's feast. They've eaten, and they're melancholy. As they cross the square heading back to their homes and the poorhouse:*)

A TALL PALE WOMAN
The instant you finish eating, all that lies ahead of you is days of not enough to eat.

A POOR WOMAN WITH A BABY
It was a decent meal, though they made such a fuss you'd think we were each getting a whole calf.

A VERY OLD POOR WOMAN
To me it's no matter. I only eat now to make of myself a bigger meal for the worms . . .

A VERY HOMELY MAN
The bride disappeared. And did you notice they'd cut each roll in half?

A POOR WOMAN WITH A BABY
He's the richest Chasid in the district, and he couldn't manage a whole roll for each guest. The rich guests got rolls.

A VERY HOMELY MAN
The rich guests got geese, and lamb, and clear broth.

A VERY OLD POOR WOMAN
I had a nice fast dance with the bride. A strange girl. Sitting next to me at the table was the Prophet Elijah. Dressed for the poorhouse. He ate and left. I'll be dead soon. God willing.

(It has gotten very dark. The lights in the shops and taverns and houses are going out. In the synagogue, as the poor cross the square, someone is lighting many candles, and many candles are lit in Sender's home. Sender, Gitl and Bessye come out on Sender's porch, looking anxiously into the gathering dark.)

SENDER

Where on earth is my daughter? What could be keeping her, what could she be thinking? And Fradde, a responsible woman! How can a visit to a graveyard take so long? They should be back, God forbid anything's happened.

BESSYE

There they are!

GITL

Let's go meet them!

(Fradde enters the square, and behind her, Leah.)

SENDER

Well *finally*!

FRADDE

Oh Sender, forgive me, we're so terribly sorry, I'll never listen to your daughter again!

SENDER

What happened to you?

(Women come out of Sender's house, including Mrs. Nachman.)

MRS. NACHMAN

The bride must come in now, she has to bless the Shabbes candles.

(The women and Leah go inside. Fradde talks to Bessye and Gitl.)

FRADDE
She fainted. Look! I'm still shaking from the fright, I tried to wake her, I thought she'd died.

BESSYE
She's fasting, she fasts all the time now, she's weak and she faints a lot.

FRADDE
She shouldn't fast except on her wedding day! It's like she's disappearing more and more, she's not sitting shiva, she's a bride.

GITL
Did she faint at her mother's grave?

FRADDE
No, it was another grave, unmarked, and don't ask me what happened, don't ask me what happened, don't ask me what happened, it's best not to know.

(Leah is brought from the house by the women. She's seated on a decorated chair. The klezmer orchestra strikes up wedding music. Menashe, Rabbi Mendl and Nachman enter from across the square, followed by the bridegroom's party. Menashe carries a bridal veil in his hands. He goes to Leah and places the veil atop her head, and brings it down over her face. The Messenger comes out of the synagogue.
Leah stands, tears off the bridal veil and throws it aside, pushes Menashe away, and screams:)

LEAH
You are not my bridegroom!

(Everyone is horrified. Sender, Fradde and Leah's friends rush to Leah. Sender grabs Leah.)

SENDER

Leah! My love! What's wrong?

(Leah tears free and runs to the grave of the Holy Couple. She throws herself on the grave, clawing at the earth.)

LEAH

Save me, Holy Bride and Groom!

(The others run to Leah and lift her up. She becomes wild-eyed and pulls away from them, and then screams in a strange, male voice:)

LEAH

AAAAAAAHHHHHHH! AAAAAAHHHHHHH! YOU BURIED ME! BUT NOW I'VE COME BACK TO MY BELOVED, AND I'LL NEVER LEAVE HER AGAIN!

(Sender goes to his daughter. She roars in his face:)

LEAH

MURDERER!

NACHMAN

She's gone mad!

THE MESSENGER

A dybbuk has entered the body of the bride.

Act Three

SCENE 1

Miropol; two days later. A train station near the Jewish Ghetto.
People are disembarking from a train, only just arrived. Among
them, the Messenger.

FIRST PASSENGER
It's a miracle! Two days from Krakow to Tarnopol to
Miropol! Home! In Two days! Used to take a week.

SECOND PASSENGER
And an even greater miracle! They let Jews ride the thing!

THIRD PASSENGER
I find the insistent tempo of the wheels and pistons, the
humming of the rails, the sway of the cabin and the hiss of
the steam extraordinarily conducive to contemplation, and
to prayer. I prayed all the way from Cheroszchev.

FIRST PASSENGER
From such an invention, only good can ever come.

THE MESSENGER
Blessed be He from whom all inventions come.

SECOND PASSENGER
So how goes it with a Jew?

THE MESSENGER
So how should it go?

SECOND PASSENGER
So what brings you to Miropol? You're not a Chasid.

THE MESSENGER
Just a messenger. At the house of your Rabbi Azriel . . .

THIRD PASSENGER
Of Blessed Name.

FIRST PASSENGER
A righteous man, a tzaddik.

THE MESSENGER
. . . a girl has been brought, possessed by a dybbuk.

THIRD PASSENGER
Sssshhhhhhhh!

SECOND PASSENGER
Oh, preposterous!

THIRD PASSENGER
Don't speak of such things in public! They won't let us ride
the train if they hear us talking about . . .

SECOND PASSENGER
And you believe that stuff? A dybbuk? And to see that, you came all the way from . . . let me guess. Minsk.

THE MESSENGER
Much farther than Minsk.

SECOND PASSENGER
Farther than Minsk! You've wasted your time and your money. God save the credulous. A dybbuk! He rode the train to see the dybbuk!

FIRST PASSENGER
Ever been to Moscow?

THE MESSENGER
(Shaking his head) Not on my route.

FIRST PASSENGER
In Moscow now they have electric lighting! And fantastically long wires, threads of fire, just like in the legends, radiant threads stretching from Moscow to St. Petersburg! Along which words fly, faster than the angels fly, over the earth, words of electric fire, like chittering crickets, can you imagine.

THIRD PASSENGER
When Moshiach comes He will arrive by train, with a first-class ticket.

FIRST PASSENGER
And light in the evening, electrical light.

SECOND PASSENGER
Soon we won't need candles anymore. In a world without candles, there will be no more dybbuks. There will be fewer hysterical women. With dybbuks, it's always women, have

you noticed?

THE MESSENGER

If you say so. It is hard for me to believe such things are possible. But I have never been to Moscow. Which way to Rabbi Azriel's house?

THIRD PASSENGER

Go first to the ghetto. You can find it by the smell. Anyone there will direct you.

SECOND PASSENGER

I hate the smell of candle smoke. Give me electric light. In a world of electric light, even Jews can ride the trains.

SCENE 2

A large room in Rabbi Azriel's house. On the right is a door leading to other rooms. Near the door is a small Holy Ark and a reading stand. On the rear wall, the front door of the house is flanked by benches and windows. To the left is a broad table. At the head of the table is an armchair. Near the Ark are a small table, a sofa and reading chairs.

Rabbi Azriel of Miropol sits in the armchair, facing the outside door. Michl, the gabbe (manager), stands at the table behind the armchair. At a table nearby sits a young man, the Scribe of Rabbi Azriel, who records the proceeding of the court in a book. Sender and Fradde stand inside near the door. Leah stands at the threshold, refusing to enter the room.

It's Saturday night, shortly after the maariv (evening prayers)

SENDER

Leah, have pity on your miserable father, don't shame him before the rabbi.

FRADDE

Please Leah, obey your father, come into the room.

LEAH

I want to but I can't.

RABBI AZRIEL

Leah! I order you to enter!

(Leah enters and goes to the Rabbi's table.)

RABBI AZRIEL

Sit down.

(Leah sits, but almost immediately jumps up again and shouts in the male voice:)

LEAH

Leave me in peace! I don't want to be here!

(Leah tries to run to the front door, but Sender and Fradde grab her.)

RABBI AZRIEL

Dybbuk, I command you: Tell me who you are.

THE DYBBUK

Rabbi of Miropol! You know all too well who I am! The others don't need my name.

RABBI AZRIEL

I ask not for your name, Dybbuk: Who are you?

(Little pause.)

THE DYBBUK

A wanderer. Who once sought a new road.

RABBI AZRIEL

There's only one road and that is righteousness.

THE DYBBUK

Too narrow! It would not take me where I belonged. There are other roads, for larger souls than yours.

RABBI AZRIEL

And you roamed those roads. With your large soul. And couldn't find your way home again. But you know the Torah: the dead may not dwell among the living.

THE DYBBUK

I never died!

RABBI AZRIEL

You have, and you must leave the body of this girl.

THE DYBBUK

I am her bridegroom; God ordained this; we are meant to be.

RABBI AZRIEL

Listen to me, wanderer: you have died, and only after the Holy Shofar is sounded on the great and terrible day of Judgment, of Wrath and Awe, only then may you return to the daylight world. Now leave her body: you blight a living branch of the eternal tree of the people Israel.

THE DYBBUK

Rabbi of Miropol! I've heard the stories about your strength! Command the angels to circle overhead, but you cannot shackle me! I've no place else to go, every ascent is barred, every doorway bolted against me! I can only fall from here into the hands of waiting demons. I cannot leave!

(Leah kneels before the Rabbi.)

THE DYBBUK

There is heaven and there is earth and there are uncountable worlds throughout the universe but nowhere, anywhere is there a resting place for me. I've found shelter, here, and you want to drive me out into the night. Have mercy, have pity on me, don't banish me.

RABBI AZRIEL

Homeless one, I do pity you, your suffering shreds my heart, and if I can I will rescue you, from the demons and from the Devil himself. But you must leave the body of the girl.

THE DYBBUK

I WILL NEVER LEAVE!

RABBI AZRIEL

Go, Michl, send to the synagogue, ask Rabbi Shimshin to come to me. Find a quorum of men and bring them here.

(Michl exits.)

RABBI AZRIEL

Dybbuk! Soul of a man who has left this world! I, Azriel, son of my righteous mother Hadas, order you to leave the body of the girl Leah, daughter of Channa, and I order you to harm no living creature as you depart! If you comply, I will protect you from the Sitra-Achra—my power can accomplish that. Refuse me, and I will blast you with curses and the awful power of God, I will with my outstretched arm hurl anathema at you and leave you to your unimaginable fate alone on the Other Side.

THE DYBBUK

(Screaming) Nothing can expel me! No power rescue me! No heaven is worth more to me than here where I am! No hell half as terrible as leaving her!

SENDER

(With supplicant arms) Rabbi, tzaddik, my daughter, help me, save her, she's my only child!

RABBI AZRIEL
What is this, Sender? How did this come to pass?

SENDER
Two days ago, just as the bridegroom placed the veil on her head, she . . .

RABBI AZRIEL
That's not the question and you know it. Through what flaw did the Evil One gain entrance?

SENDER
Rabbi, I swear my Leah is a pure and decent Jewish girl, she . . .

RABBI AZRIEL
The Lord visits his wrath across generations.

(Sender looks at the Scribe, who is busy writing.)

SENDER
Rabbi, must this boy write down everything we say?

RABBI AZRIEL
He must! Yes, absolutely, we record the nocturnal doings of God the same as the miracles and blessings He bestows; the tales of the dybbukim are as important as the legends of the tzaddikim, and as instructive. It may be that your daughter suffers this evil impregnation simply so that we may turn her sufferings into a text—for others to study in the ages to come. Or it may be that she suffers for some other reason. Children sometimes bear the punishment for their parents' wickedness.

SENDER
Don't you think I haven't asked myself a dozen times every minute: What have I done to God that suddenly He

should hate me so ferociously He would smite my only joy
with . . .

RABBI AZRIEL

Have you asked the dybbuk?

SENDER

You can't ask him anything, he only rages and snarls.

THE DYBBUK

MURDERER!

SENDER

You see?

THE DYBBUK

EVIL ANCIENT MURDERER! WHAT I'M SUFFERING
MAY YOU ENDURE A THOUSANDFOLD! MAY YOU
NEVER FIND REST! MAY YOUR MONEY POISON
YOUR BLOOD!

SENDER

I recognize his voice, it belonged to a yeshiva student who
studied in Brinnitz, he perished in shul a few months ago.
He'd profaned, he was studying forbidden things, his soul
had grown rusted and corroded, deformed.

RABBI AZRIEL

How is it you know so intimately the state of his soul?

SENDER

Right before he died, Rabbi, he told a fellow student
that sin came from God, God help us, that we weakened
ourselves fighting the devil. He was an alchemist, he read
the Zohar, the Book of Raziel which Adam mislaid, he
would chew and swallow scraps of paper inscribed with

spells, he made a strange powder by crushing pearls and he recited the seven colors of gold, he told his friend he was making gold coins for some wicked old miser.

RABBI AZRIEL
You knew this student well, Sender?

SENDER
No, he was occasionally a guest at my table for Shabbes, I've always had students at my table.

RABBI AZRIEL
Think Sender, till your brains ache, did you insult this boy? Did he have bad table manners, did you mock him? Refuse him food when he was hungry?

SENDER
Never.

RABBI AZRIEL
Have you injured anyone in his family?

SENDER
I don't even know his family name, Rabbi, I never spoke to the boy, I can't remember, please help me, I'm not perfect but I'm a decent man, I . . .

RABBI AZRIEL
They tell me you don't read so much anymore, Sender; your eyes are faded from adding sums and keeping accounts.

(Michl enters with the quorum of men.)

THE DYBBUK
I WILL NOT LEAVE!

RABBI AZRIEL

(To the men of the quorum) Holy minyan. In your names and
in your powers, do you invest me with the authority to
expel from the body of this Jewish girl a spirit who refuses
to leave her of its own free will?

THE MINYAN

(Unison) In our names and in our powers we invest you,
Rabbi Azriel, with the authority to expel from the body of
this Jewish girl a spirit who refuses to leave her of its own
free will.

(The Rabbi stands.)

RABBI AZRIEL

In the name of Almighty God, I beseech you, one last
time, leave the body of this girl. If you refuse me I will
excommunicate you and bind your soul over to the angels
of destruction.

(A terrifying pause.)

THE DYBBUK

In the name of God Almighty, I am with my intended now,
and I will never leave her.

RABBI AZRIEL

Michl. Bring a white robe for every person in the room,
seven rams' horns and seven black candles.

(Michl goes into the inner room.)

LEAH

(As if waking, in her own voice) Fradde! What are they doing
to him? What are they going to do to me?

FRADDE

Hush, child, the rabbi only wishes you well.

SENDER

Rabbi Azriel is among the holiest of men, Leah, he . . .

LEAH

Fradde, please, tell him . . . I want to leave here . . . Don't tell him anything. Tell him to leave me alone.

FRADDE

Sleep, my poor child, close your eyes. The rabbi's very wise and only good can come from him.

LEAH

Hold me, Fradde . . .

FRADDE

I *can't,* my only love. You terrify me . . .

(Michl returns, carrying the rams' horns and the candles. Behind him, the Messenger carries the white robes. Behind them is Rabbi Shimshin.)

RABBI SHIMSHIN

A good week, blessed Rebbe.

RABBI AZRIEL

(Standing) And a good year, Rabbi. Michl has told you . . . ?

RABBI SHIMSHIN

He has.

RABBI AZRIEL

The spirit refuses to abdicate, there's no choice but to drive him out this girl, violently. Before I proceed, you, as

Chief Rabbi of Miropol, must give your consent, and the
mitzvah of sparing her young life will shine in your crown
in heaven.

RABBI SHIMSHIN
Rabbi, I am your disciple in all things, but excommunication
is a terrible fate for a Jewish soul, and Rabbi . . . When
Michl told me what had befallen Sender's daughter I was
only very frightened, not surprised, because in this past
week I have had three dreams which clearly pertain to this
case.

RABBI AZRIEL
If we are to perform this ceremony, Rabbi Shimshin, it must
be done before midnight as you know, and . . . There is a
danger here. The child is dying. The dybbuk is drawing
away her life.

RABBI SHIMSHIN
I cannot consent to an exorcism until we speak.

(Little pause.)

RABBI AZRIEL
(To Michl:) Rabbi Shimshin and I will confer.
(Turning to the minyan) Pray to the Blessed Name for mercy,
or wisdom, or protection; do not touch the girl or let her
touch you.

*(Azriel takes Shimshin aside. They confer in whispers.
The minyan begins its prayers, everyone shukkeling. The First
Chasid stops and says:)*

FIRST CHASID
I can't pray. I am afraid.

SECOND CHASID

Pray anyway. If you pray, the Holy One, Blessed be He, may preserve you from Evil; if Evil overtakes you, it's better that it overtake you while you're praying.

THIRD CHASID

So said my rabbi while they were burning our village. Every murdered man was found wearing his tefilin and talis. We buried them that way, in a big hasty pit. And then we fled into the forests. It was night, I was a child, I remember owls screeching.

FIRST CHASID

The darkness and misery of the world is incomprehensible to me. I cannot pray.

THIRD CHASID

The world is in its last age. If Moshiach doesn't come soon there'll be no Jews left to welcome Him.

(Azriel and Shimshin cease their conference.)

RABBI AZRIEL

Take the girl to a room.

FRADDE

Rabbi, I am terribly afraid, she's cold, and hardly breathing, and she won't open her eyes.

RABBI AZRIEL

The room is cold, the world is cold, its variety is deceptive, there's not so much to see. Heaven preserve her.

(Fradde leads Leah out, accompanied by Michl.)

SENDER
Where's she going? Rabbi, why aren't you . . .

RABBI AZRIEL
(To the minyan) Everyone, retire to my study. Pray. This house must vibrate to the sound of praying. I will call you in an hour.

(The minyan leaves. Rabbi Shimshin notices the Scribe, who is writing everything down.)

RABBI SHIMSHIN
If these proceedings are being recorded, the scribe should wear an amulet or a tefilin on his arm as he writes. In Baghdad only recently the scribes who made the records of the dybbuk infestation that was the false messiah, Sabbathai Zvi . . .

(Everyone except Azriel spits.)

RABBI SHIMSHIN
The scribes themselves became possessed by the false messiah, merely by writing the letters of his name.

RABBI AZRIEL
Almighty God, assist me, I'm your servant, don't hinder me, strengthen me. I will proceed towards that which I know to be Just. Illumine this night. Do not leave me in such blindness. Sender?

SENDER
Yes, Rebbe?

RABBI AZRIEL
Have you remembered anything, Sender, about this dead boy, anything that might help save your daughter?

SENDER

Rebbe, I can't think clearly, I . . .

RABBI AZRIEL

Sender surely you remember a young Chasid from Brinnitz who twenty years ago studied here with you? Nissin ben Rivka was his name.
(Little pause.)

SENDER

Nissin died, Rebbe.

RABBI SHIMSHIN

That is true.

RABBI AZRIEL

I remember him, Sender. You were the closest of friends.

SENDER

Nissin moved far away, Rebbe, we lost touch, and I heard he died young.

RABBI SHIMSHIN

For three nights Nissin has appeared to me in my dreams.

SENDER

He's dead.

RABBI SHIMSHIN

Nissin ben Rivka has appeared imploring me to bring Sender of Brinnitz before a Rabbinical Court. Nissin said Sender had spilled Nissin's blood.

SENDER

Lies! I've taken nothing of his! He has no claim on anything that's mine!

RABBI SHIMSHIN

The dead boy who has become a dybbuk is Nissin's son.
(Pause.)

SENDER

(Broken, to Azriel) Rebbe, advise me, tell me what I should
do.

RABBI AZRIEL

We will summon the righteous dead man Nissin ben Rivka
to present his charges before our court. It's his right as a
Jew. You'll hear the charges brought before the court, what
else Sender. You have no right to refuse. Sender?

SENDER

I obey.

RABBI AZRIEL

You summoned the bridegroom and his family, Sender?

SENDER

Rebbe, I think the bridegroom's family is having second
thoughts about being my in-laws. I think they will refuse
to come.

RABBI AZRIEL

I ORDER THEM TO BE HERE, I COMMAND IT! *(Roaring
at Sender!)* HAAAAAAA! The bridegroom must be here!

(The Messenger enters.)

THE MESSENGER

The bridegroom will arrive in time.

(Rabbi Azriel looks at the Messenger.)

RABBI AZRIEL
There's a stranger in our midst.

SENDER
He's a messenger, Rebbe, he . . . *(To the Messenger)* You were there, that night, when . . .

RABBI AZRIEL
Has he delivered his message, Sender?

SENDER
I . . . I don't know, Rabbi, I . . . Should I ask him to leave, Rabbi?

RABBI AZRIEL
God forbid! Welcome the outsider, offer him a chair.

SENDER
No, Rebbe, this man is strange, I think he . . .

RABBI AZRIEL
Sender . . . Can a few short years really have changed a man so much?
(To the Messenger, gesturing to Sender) You see how frail we are?
(To Sender) You don't welcome the stranger, you remember nothing, you question nothing, you're joyless . . .

SENDER
Joyless? My daughter is destroyed, everything I worked for is destroyed, of course I'm joyless! From what conceivable cause in the world might joy come to . . .

RABBI AZRIEL
Sender! Who made the World?

SENDER

What? Rabbi, please, I don't know what you're asking, I'm .
. . miserable, Rebbe, don't ask me difficult questions.

RABBI AZRIEL

Who made the world is a difficult question?

(Little pause.)

SENDER

Please, Rebbe. I am a heartbroken man.

RABBI AZRIEL

Ssssshhh. Sender. I gave you a task. Now go and do what
I say.

*(Sender exits. Rabbi Azriel turns to the Messenger. They stare at
one another; the Messenger smiles. The Rabbi asks him:)*

RABBI AZRIEL

So who made the World?

THE MESSENGER

God made the World.

RABBI AZRIEL

The world is Holy because it is from God.

THE MESSENGER

The world is holy because it is from God.

RABBI AZRIEL

So simple. So wonderful. And yet . . . *(Indicating the direction
in which Sender has exited)* You see . . . ? Not so simple.
Which is the Holiest of lands?

THE MESSENGER

The Holy Land.

RABBI AZRIEL

The Holiest City?

THE MESSENGER

Jerusalem.

RABBI AZRIEL

The Temple in Jerusalem was the Holiest place, and the Holiest room was?

THE MESSENGER

The Holy of Holies.

RABBI AZRIEL

There are seventy nations, and which is Holiest?

THE MESSENGER

The people Israel.
Of the twelve tribes of Israel the Holiest is Levi,
Of the Levites the Holiest are the priests,
And the Holiest of these is the High Priest of Israel.

RABBI AZRIEL

Three hundred and fifty-four are the days of the year, and which is Holiest?

THE MESSENGER

Yom Kippur.

RABBI AZRIEL

And which is the Holiest Yom Kippur?

THE MESSENGER
When Yom Kippur falls on Shabbes.

RABBI AZRIEL
Seventy languages are spoken on earth and the Holiest is
Hebrew. That Hebrew is Holiest which is found . . . ?

THE MESSENGER
In the Torah.

RABBI AZRIEL
In the Torah which is the Holiest text?

THE MESSENGER
The Ten Commandments.

RABBI AZRIEL
And which is the Holiest word therein?

THE MESSENGER
(Softly) The Holiest word is the Shem ha-Mfoyrosh.

RABBI AZRIEL
God's own unutterable name.

(Little pause.)

And this is what everyone knows: at one instant all these
conjoin—on Yom Kippur on Shabbes the High Priest
entered the Holy of Holies and pronounced the Shem
ha-Mfoyrosh, the Tetragrammaton: Yud, Hey, Vov, Hey.
At that moment of complete and absolute holiness, had
a single thought of sin, God forbid, a machshovve zorre,
entered the mind of the High Priest, the world would
have died. Wheresoever a man raises his eyes to heaven,

that is the Holy of Holies. Every person created by God, b'tsalmoy uchd'musoy, in His image, is High Priest. Every day of our lives is The Day of Atonement, every day is the Holy Shabbes day, every word spoken without malice is the Shem ha-Vawyaw, the name of God. Therefore, as everyone knows, every sin committed or imagined, every injustice destroys the world. Every word, every thought, every instant of every day. If all comes to rest . . .

(The Messenger lightly touches the nape of the Rabbi's neck.)

RABBI AZRIEL
Yes, there. When a soul falls, when it stumbles under the weight, from the lips of every angel, the Matriarchs and Patriarchs, every tzaddik, from every Holy Ark in every Temple, even from the Almighty Himself, dark lamentations issue forth, drowning the world in woe.
It's a great burden, don't you think? For the joyless and the frail.

THE MESSENGER
The soul is drawn to the Divine Fire like a baby to its mother's breast, but even as it reaches the highest spheres, the Evil One may emerge and, God help his children, the soul will plummet, and of course if it has soared high it will have that much farther to fall.

RABBI AZRIEL
God made the World.

THE MESSENGER
The World id Holy, because it is from God.

THE SCRIBE
I beg your pardon, Rebbe, but last night I had bad dreams, and tonight after Shabbes prayers I found that somehow

all my pens were ruined overnight, and now, when I try
to write down what you say, the paper won't take the ink.

RABBI AZRIEL

(To the Scribe) Later, perhaps, we'll interpret your dreams
and buy new pens and paper. It's all been written before,
everything we do and say, it's all in some scroll, some
codex, some tractate or holy book—Jews have merely
tumbled from the pages of books, what we speak and think
has all been written by the Hand of God. From whence
comes our joy.

*(Offstage, the sonorous sound of a large number of men praying
together. Amidst the prayers, a terrible wailing sound, equally
balanced between grief and rage. A cantor is heard, keening a
prayer.)*

RABBI AZRIEL

Suddenly I am enormously weary.

RABBI SHIMSHIN

The task of summoning a dead man to Rabbinical Court is
very difficult, and very dangerous, and only someone as
mighty in his faith as you are could attempt it, Holy Azriel.

RABBI AZRIEL

(To the Scribe) Write the Sh'ma and the blessings, over and
over, till we return, and do not look up from the Book. If a
strange thought enters you as you labor, do not dismiss it
but write it down. Begin with the bad dream you had last
night. And then write Chelmo tovo chozze.

THE SCRIBE

Chelmo tovo chozze.

RABBI SHIMSHIN
Chelmo tovo chazeyso. We have dreamt good dreams.

(As the Scribe writes and mutters the prayers:)

RABBI AZRIEL
I am very weary, and I'm very weak, and older than my days, I have been Rebbe for more than forty years and there are many days when the Almighty hides from me, and I pray to a void, to a fear. I want to seek after my elusive God in silence and contemplation, but there are always petitioners at my door, even on the bad days when I am abandoned and empty. Many generations have passed since the Temple fell, and I am as many miles from the source of Life, and I wither and pale . . .

(Little pause.)

MICHL
Your grandfather was a disciple of the Baal Shem Tov, Rebbe, your father was a tzaddik, and there are generations behind them of wise men and saints, and these all stand behind you, Rabbi Azriel, they guard and fortify you, as they always have. Your holy father Ishtele saw the Prophet Elijah, three times. When Mayer Ber your uncle recited the Sh'ma Yisroel he would rise to the ceiling of the shul and sometimes he floated up to Heaven, and the great Velvele your blessed grandfather brought the dead to life.

RABBI AZRIEL
Do you know, Michl, how my grandfather drove out dybbuks? He'd bellow, "HAAAAAAA!" No words or prayers or minyans. He'd simply yell at a dybbuk and the dybbuk went. "HAAAAAAAAA!"
Of course the rabbis were all much mightier back then.
(He looks up to Heaven for a moment, and then says to Shimshin

and Michl) We must prepare ourselves. Go inside. I'll join you in a moment.

(Shimshin and Michl withdraw.)

RABBI AZRIEL

(To the air) Holy Velvele, you stand behind this chair and grip my shoulders! You have been dead sixty-seven years; in that time I only grow weaker, and the world grows wickeder. But you in Paradise have grown stronger, and I ask you to accompany me now. In Lublin, in Zlotchov, pogroms. The people talk idly of traveling and scientific marvels and don't pray. I'm older than my years, I don't sleep at night. Under my robe, my knees knock together in fear sometimes. *(Softly)* And sometimes, Grandfather, I do not entirely trust God. *(To the Scribe)* Don't write that down.

Act Four

An hour later. The same room as Act Three. Where the broad Sabbath dining table stood there is a now a smaller table, behind which are Rabbi Azriel's armchair flanked by three smaller chairs. Rabbi Azriel and the two other Rabbinical Judges are seated in the armchair and two of the smaller chairs, in prayer shawls and phylacteries. Rabbi Shimshin, similarly attired, is standing at one end of the table. Michl stands in attendance, the Scribe is writing furiously. In one corner a curtain is hanging. The men are praying together in Hebrew. The sounds of prayers continue to come from the adjoining rooms. Azriel says:

RABBI AZRIEL

Ohmayn.

(He stands and, holding a long cane, he walks to the curtain. Drawing from left to right Azriel makes a circle on the floor with his cane, saying:)

RABBI AZRIEL

We summon Nissin ben Rivka now to appear before the Rabbinical Court. Nissin I will command you to appear with in this circle behind this curtain we have hung for you, for your modesty and for our protection; you may not leave it. Sender!

SENDER

Yes Rabbi?

RABBI AZRIEL

We have summoned the righteous dead man Nissin. Will you accept our judgment?

SENDER

I will accept it.

RABBI AZRIEL

And comply with its every demand?

SENDER

I'll do what I am told.

RABBI AZRIEL

Good. Go stand over there.

SENDER

I've thought through the night, Rabbi, I didn't sleep, and I remember something, a pact I made with Nissin, which I have broken but . . .

RABBI AZRIEL

(Clapping his hands with impatient anger!) Sender! Sender! Sender! I am not your teacher and you are not my pupil anymore! Now go stand where I tell you. Await the plaintiff and the presentation of his complaint.

SENDER
(As he goes to the spot the Rabbi had indicated) But I broke it in genuine ignorance, and this is perhaps . . .

RABBI AZRIEL
Ssssshhhhhh!

(Everyone is silent.)

RABBI AZRIEL
A being from the True World is about to enter this room, to our world, the world of Illusion, to demand of us that we settle his grievance against this man through strict application of the laws of the Torah, which as this trial proves governs not only the world but all the universe.
(Pause)
The trial will be watched by the heavens, by their entire populations; wheels and dominions, the zazahot and the ten sefirot; one of their citizens has come to us for Justice. We are in danger, therefore, for no deviation from the law is permitted, and the censure is destruction. And so as all judges must, we sit in the awful majesty of the law, full of fear.

THE FIRST RABBINICAL JUDGE
The plaintiff is here, Rabbi. I've grown cold . . .

THE SECOND RABBINICAL JUDGE
And I smell earth, and ash. I taste metal on my tongue.

THE SCRIBE
(Chanting softly in Hebrew as he writes) N'vakeysh et nitzotzot hanefesh matzitey m'orey ha'eysh. N'haleyl et nishmat kol chay unvareych al miney b'samim.

RABBI SHIMSHIN

(Over the above) I believe Nissin has come.

RABBI AZRIEL

Righteous dead man, Nissin ben Rivka, do you agree to stay within the circle the Rabbinical Court has prepared for you? And will you obey our command and tell the Rabbinical Court your complaint against Sender ben Henya?

(A terrifying pause, and silence; all listen, petrified.)

THE FIRST RABBINICAL JUDGE

I hear a chanting, keening voice without words.

THE SECOND RABBINICAL JUDGE

Before my eyes I see an ancient hand scribing letters, but I hear nothing!

THE SCRIBE

(In a huge voice) N'VAREYCH ET EYN HACHAYIM, M'KOR HAVCHANAH! NIZKEH NA L'HAVIN ULHASKIL, LISHOMO'A, LIMOD UL'LAMEYD, LISHMOR V'LA'ASOT ULKAYEYM DIVREY TORAH B'AHAVAH.

RABBI SHIMSHIN

(To Sender) Sender ben Henya. The righteous dead man Nissin ben Rivka claims the following against you: You were both young men in this yeshiva years ago, you were true friends; once during the Days of Awe, when all oaths are especially sacrosanct, you vowed that your love for one another and the union of your souls would one day become flesh. When the women you married had conceived, if the Almighty would make one bear a daughter and one bear a

son, these your children would become husband and wife. You vowed this to each other, you swore before . . .

SENDER

We did, I suppose, we . . . Yes, but it was terribly long ago and then he . . .

RABBI SHIMSHIN

The righteous dead man claims that after he had left Miropol and traveled to a remote shtetl, his wife had a son and yours had a daughter.

SENDER

I had a daughter but I didn't know anything more from him, he . . .

RABBI SHIMSHIN

It was soon after his son was born that Nissin the righteous man died.

SENDER

NISSIN! I never knew you had a boy, I . . . .

THE SCRIBE

(Loud, keening) HEYEYH ASHER TIHYEH, VEHEYEYH BARUCH BA'ASHER TIHYEH!

RABBI SHIMSHIN

AND I LEARNED . . . THAT MY SON . . . HAD A BLESSED SOUL . . . EXALTED, HE . . . ROSE LIKE A FALCON IN THE MOUNTAINS, HIGHER, HIGHER, TOUCHING CLOUDS, I WAS . . . VERY PROUD.
(Pause)
But my boy . . . wandered . . . town to town, crossing borders, for his soul . . . KNEW, IT WAS SEEKING! WHAT

YOU AND I HAD VOWED! HIS . . . Beloved. Intended.
(Pause)
And he found her at your house, Sender, at your table.
(Little pause)
But Nissin's son was a poor student and you Sender, you
are a rich man. So you ignored your daughter's destined
bridegroom, you searched elsewhere for your son-in-law .
. . This horror has come . . . AND MORE WILL COME . . .
Because you are a dishonest! Desperate! Greedy Man! MY
SON MEANWHILE . . . BURNED!
He wandered . . . again but now . . . BLIND, in despair! The
new paths he sought led to dark places, AND I . . . COULD
NOT WARN HIM! Till the boy fell prey to the Sitra-Achra
and its light-devouring false beauty, to the demons that
dragged him untimely from the world.
(Little pause)
And now: Nissin's son has become a dybbuk min ha-
hizonim, and his soul has stolen into the body of his
beloved.
(Little pause)
Nissin ben Rivka claims before this Court: His son is
dead, his wife dead too, and now his own name is not
remembered by anyone, he has no grandchildren now nor
ever will, and no one says Kaddish for Nissin ben Rivka.
His light, his best loved child, has died now for all eternity.
He asks of the Court this judgment of Sender ben Henya:
Sender has spilled the blood of Nissin's son, and his son's
children, and theirs, and theirs, until the End of Days.

(Pause. Sender weeps.)

RABBI AZRIEL
Sender ben Henya, you've heard the charges the righteous
dead man has brought. How do you answer?

SENDER

I can barely speak.

(Little pause)

Nissin my old friend, I can't justify this terrible wrong or undo the evil that's been done already, but it was a sin committed ignorantly, not because I bore anyone malice, you least of all. Nissin you moved away after that Yom Kippur when we made our vows, and I didn't know you'd had a son. I never heard from you again. Years passed before I learned you'd died.

RABBI AZRIEL

Did you send after him? Try to learn where he'd gone, investigate?

SENDER

Years passed. Day by day, I simply forgot.

(Little pause.)

RABBI SHIMSHIN

Nissin ben Rivka would like to know—Sender: Why you never asked his son, who was a visitor at your table many times, what his name was or what town he was from?

SENDER

I don't . . . that was a long time ago, too, I can't remember now; don't suspect my motives, Nissin, you were the bridegroom's father, it was your job to approach me and anyway, look at how I tried to keep her unmarried, I was impossible with the marriage terms, I kept three suitors away from her because in my heart I knew someone would come for her, your son, but . . . Finally, this last suitor, his family's powerful and compliant and . . .

RABBI SHIMSHIN

I . . . SUSPECT your motives, and your heart, SENDER . . .
because in the heart within the heart within you knew who
this boy was . . . who resembled his father so strongly . . .
YOU DID NOT ASK WHO HIS FATHER WAS BECAUSE
YOU DIDN'T WANT TO KNOW.
To make your daughter rich and comfortable, you exiled
his son to a demon-haunted abyss.

(Pause.)

RABBI AZRIEL

We will render our decision now.

(The Rabbis confer while Sender covers his face, weeping quietly.)

RABBI AZRIEL

The Rabbinical Court, its power descending from
God, having listened to both parties, has decided this:
Something that has not been created cannot be bound up
in an oath, and since we do not know if conception had
taken place in either wife when the vows were made, it
cannot be determined if the vows were binding here on
earth. Nevertheless, the heavens must have accepted these
vows, for Nissin's son knew of the promise in his heart,
and sought his bride; and furthermore great tragedy has
resulted from Sender's failure to keep honor with his
friend. It is thus the judgment of the Rabbinical Court that,
since the absolute truth is caught halfway between this
world and the next, Sender must give half of all he has
to the poor; not a kopek less than half. And for the rest of
his life Sender is to burn yahrzeit candles and recite the
mourner's Kaddish each year for Nissin ben Rivka and for
Nissin's son. As if these dead were of his own family.
(Little pause)
The Rabbinical Court asks the righteous dead man

Nissin ben Rivka to forgive Sender completely and for all eternity, and at the same time to use his paternal authority to command his son to leave the body of Sender's daughter Leah; for if he doesn't he will kill a living branch of the people Israel. Help us, Nissin, and the Almighty will then show his vast grace to Nissin, and to his homeless son.

THE MESSENGER

AMEN!

RABBI AZRIEL

Nissin ben Rivka, have you heard the judgment of this Court and do you accept it?

(A fearful pause)

Do you accept our judgment?

(A fearful pause)

I, Azriel, son of Ishtele son of Velvele command you Righteous dead man Nissin ben Rivka to answer me!

(Silence)

Sender ben Henya, have you heard the judgment of this Court and do you accept it?

SENDER

I . . . I accept. Yes, but he . . . .

RABBI AZRIEL

Righteous dead man Nissin ben Rivka, the litigation is ended now between you and Sender ben Henya. You must return to your realm, the True World, and we enjoin you to forebear hurting any living creature as you leave. Michl! Remove the curtain, clear a space in the room, and send for water! And tell the minyan to prepare itself!

(Michl goes to the door, opens it, says something to a servant outside, and then removes the curtain. Rabbi Azriel draws the

circle with his cane again, but this time right to left, and a servant enters with water and a pitcher. Everyone washes their hands as the other three Rabbis talk in whispers:)

RABBI SHIMSHIN
The dead man didn't forgive Sender.

THE FIRST RABBINICAL JUDGE
I know. What can that mean?

THE SECOND RABBINICAL JUDGE
And the dead man didn't say he accepted the judgment.

RABBI SHIMSHIN
Or say Amen to Rebbe Azriel's conclusion. Nissin's hatred must be very hot and inextinguishable. I think something terrible is coming.

THE FIRST RABBINICAL JUDGE
Rabbi Azriel is frightened, his hands shake.

THE SECOND RABBINICAL JUDGE
This is an ill-omened Court, and my business here is through.

(The First and Second Rabbinical Judges leave furtively.)

RABBI AZRIEL
(To Sender) Is the bridegroom here yet?

SENDER
I haven't heard their carriage, Rebbe.

RABBI AZRIEL
Go send another rider to hasten them on their way, what's keeping them? See that the preparations are made for the

wedding in the shul, a canopy, musicians, tell them to be
ready to play loudly, and bring in the bride. She's been
dressed in her bridal gown?

(Sender nods.)

RABBI AZRIEL

Go! Go!
(Removing his prayer shawl and phylacteries) Lord of Creation,
King of the Universe, do You amuse Yourself? At my
expense? Very well, laugh, Blessed name! But I swear before
you I will undo this pact, even if it was pledged at the foot
of Your Throne, I will tear these two asunder, it is Unholy!
If I am wrong, break me like a bottle, but I will work this
wonder in Your Name!

*(Sender and Fradde lead Leah in. She is dressed again in her
wedding gown, with a black cloak over that. She is seated on the
sofa. Shimshin stands next to Azriel.)*

RABBI AZRIEL

Dybbuk! In the name of the Chief Rabbi of Miropol, in the
names of a holy minyan of Jews, in the name of the august
Sanhedrin in Jerusalem, I, Azriel ben Hadas, command
you a final time: Leave the body of this girl!

THE DYBBUK

I CANNOT! I WILL NEVER LEAVE!

RABBI AZRIEL

Michl, open the inner doors.

*(Michl does so, and fourteen men enter in white robes, each
carrying either a ram's horn or black candle.)*

RABBI AZRIEL

Open the Ark. Remove the Torahs.

(Michl opens the Ark and removes seven scrolls, which are handed to seven of the minyan.)

RABBI AZRIEL

Wicked and obdurate spirit, ru'ah tezazit, Dybbuk me-ru'ah ra'ah, having defied my decree and my authority, I must now call Metatron and the Kerubim, Raphael, Michael, Gabriel and Sandalphon, the mightiest of the angels, all praises be, to marshall the spirits of the upper air to pry you loose from this living child.
Blow the horns! TEKIAH!

(The men blow their horns, "TEKIAH!"
Leah screams, leaps up; Sender and Fradde try to hold her but she pushes them away, and then falls and writhes on the ground.)

THE DYBBUK

LEAVE ME! LEAVE ME! DON'T PULL ME AWAY! I DON'T WANT TO GO! I CAN'T! I CAN'T!

RABBI AZRIEL

Since you have not submitted to the upper air, I next call on the Shedim Yehuda'im, demons submissive to the Almighty Torah, demons of the middle air, caught between worlds, between good and evil, I place you under their savage authority, and let their iron claws tear you away! Blow the horns. SHVORIM!

(Again the horns blast, "SHVORIM!"
Leah writhes and the Dybbuk shouts, but with waning strength:)

THE DYBBUK

OH Most High, Holy King, all the powers of creation have turned against me! Demons and angels and a host of righteous souls, souls, and my father is with them, and they command me to go, their voices are thunder, ice and

searing heat, but I defy you all! Kill me if you want me
gone but while I have strength I WILL NOT LET GO!

RABBI AZRIEL
(To himself, shaken) Something powerful is helping him!

(Pause. Then the Rabbi says to Michl, quietly:)

RABBI AZRIEL
Michl, put the Torahs back in the Ark.

(Michl and the other men do this.)

RABBI AZRIEL
Shroud the Ark in black.

(A black cloth is placed over the Ark.)

RABBI AZRIEL
Now the candles must be lit.

*(As the black candles are lit Michl helps Rabbi Azriel and Rabbi
Shimshin into white robes.*
*There is a hush in the room and Rabbi Azriel stands over the girl,
raising his arm and intoning in a terrifying voice:)*

RABBI AZRIEL
God Almighty, rise up from your Throne, fly as a Vulture
that hastens to devour, terrible and dreadful, a leopard
and a wolf, the foaming of mighty waters, whose great day
is near, whose day of waste and desolation is near, Lord of
the Saltpits, of the breeding-place of nettles, in the name of
the Patriarchs, in the name of Matriarchs, of the martyred
and the slain, in the name of the blood of the God of Wrath
and Vengeance, I, Azriel ben Hadas, break every thread
that binds you, spirit of the dybbukim, to the world of the

living and to the body of the daughter of Channa! GO!

THE DYBBUK

(Shrieking) GOD!

RABBI AZRIEL

And from the community and the people Israel, I
anathematize and exile you! TERUAH!

THE MESSENGER

The spark shatters the vessel, and dissolves in the flame.

THE DYBBUK

I cannot . . . hold . . . I cannot hold on . . .

*(The men blast "TERUAH" on the rams' horns. The Rabbi holds
his hand up for silence.)*

RABBI AZRIEL

Dybbuk, are you slipping away?

THE DYBBUK

(Very weak) I . . . I am dying, Rebbe.

RABBI AZRIEL

Then with all my power I rescind your anathema.
(To Michl and the other men) Put out all the candles and tear
down the shroud. Hide the rams' horns. And all of you in
the minyan must leave. Michl take them out. Immediately.

*(They obey the Rabbi's instructions. The men of the quorum,
including the Messenger, and Michl as well, leave the room.)*

RABBI AZRIEL

God of Mercy and Goodness, forgive this homeless and
tormented soul, take him in Your loving hands and heal

his injuries, strike his sins from the Book of Life, and for his early life of piety and good works and great learning, for all that he has suffered, and for the righteousness of his ancestors, Lord of the Universe who alone forgives and judges, and whose compassion is infinite, save him from demons and prepare a room for his rest in Your palace of splendors. Amen.

THE MESSENGER

Amen!

(Leah shudders violently.)

THE DYBBUK

Say Kaddish for me, I am dying.

RABBI AZRIEL

Sender!

SENDER

Yisgadal ve-yiskadash shmey rabo b'olma di b'ra chirusey ... magnified and Sanctified be His Great Name throughout the World that He has created according to his Will. May He establish His kingdom in your lifetime and in your days, and in the lifetime of all the House of Israel, soon, with speed. And say Amen.

(A clock strikes twelve. Leah jumps to her feet, looking about, terror-stricken, and screams. And then she falls to the floor, unconscious.)

RABBI AZRIEL

Now we must move with haste. Take the bride to the canopy! Surely the others have finally . . .

(Michl runs in, frightened.)

MICHL

Rabbi, you must come, the bridegroom and his family are
on the outskirts of the town, their carriage lost its wheels,
their mules have died, the riders we sent after them, their
horses went wild and charged off into the night, and on
the outskirts of town all the cocks have started crowing, at
midnight, the bridegroom has fainted, they've carried him
on foot but they're suddenly so stricken with terror they
cannot take another step! You must come now!

RABBI AZRIEL

Sender! This is the golden destiny your negotiations have
bought you!

THE SCRIBE

Rabbi! I turned to a new page in your record book, and
look! It's already filled! It was pure, unwritten-upon a
moment ago, and . . .

(Little pause. The Rabbi looks at the book the Scribe's holding.)

RABBI AZRIEL

Read.

THE SCRIBE

(Reading:)

Rabbi, only turn the page:
the wonders of the coming age
will dwarf your shtetl magic so—
dybbuks, golems, all you know,
your writings and the words you say,
like oven ashes, swept away.
At some not-very-distant date
the martyred dead accumulate;

books of history will contain
mountain-piles of the slain.

*(The Rabbi and the Messenger look at one another. The Rabbi nods
his head.)*

RABBI AZRIEL

What must be will be.
(To Fradde) Woman, to your loving care I entrust this bride.
(He draws a circle, right to left, around Fradde and Leah.)

Sender and Michl you will come with me.
(To the Scribe) Write nothing further of the events of this
night. Take what you have written, wrap it in a shroud, go
to the river and drown this Book.

*(The Rabbi, the Scribe, Sender and Michl exit, leaving Fradde and
Leah alone.)*

LEAH

(Waking up) Who's here . . . ? Oh Fradde. Fradde I'm so
tired, and horribly cold; cradle me. Every limb is heavy . . .

(Fradde cradles Leah.)

FRADDE

You shouldn't feel heavy now, my darling one, my own,
let the rat feel heavy, let the cat feel heavy, you should
feel like a goosedown feather, the breath of an infant, a
snowflake, the wind in the wings of the angels . . .

LEAH

(Shuddering) Fradde I'm frightened, I hear feet drumming
the ground, they're dancing around the grave of the
Martyred Couple, they're dancing for the dead bride and
her groom.

FRADDE

Don't shiver, darling, sixty Maccabees with bronze swords
and shields surround us, the Matriarchs too, and no evil
can reach us here . . .

(She begins to sing softly:)

Soon to the canopy you will be led,
Your mother arrives from the World of the dead,
And she comes to your wedding in silver and gold,
She offers her hands for the angels to hold.
Oh Channala's daughter's a glorious bride.
Does Channala glitter with gold or with pride?
Then Channa your mother says, bursting with joy,
"My Leah is marrying a wonderful boy."
But suddenly, Channala, why do you sigh,
And why does your heart break, and why do you cry?
"Strangers are leading the bridal parade
While I stand, unseen, alone and afraid.
The living are dancing with those that they see,
And only the dead will be dancing with me."
And the daughter of Channa is married that day
To the bridegroom who's waiting to dance her away.
But
See the klezmorim, they sing and they play,
And all through the dancing, the spirits will stray,
Among them, Eliahu, he dances and sings
And silver and gold are the blessings he brings.
And shekels slop over the Prophet's gold cup,
And the living and dead rush to gobble them up . . .
Soon to the canopy you will be lead;
Your mother arrives from the world of the dead.
Amen, Amen . . .

*(Fradde lies back and quickly falls asleep; Leah too is drowsing,
when she hears a loud sigh and sits up.)*

LEAH

Who sighed so brokenly?

CHONEN'S VOICE

I did.

LEAH

I can't see you.

CHONEN'S VOICE

They've torn us apart, and around you there's a magic circle.

LEAH

Your voice is like a violin on a summer's night, playing a melody I remember . . . Who are you?

CHONEN'S VOICE

I've forgotten.
I can remember only if you remember me . . .

LEAH

I do. I remember.
On summer nights I would open the window in my room, and there was always a low bright star that burned brave and alone, it made me cry with loneliness. And then someone in my dreams came at night. And he was that horizon light. Was that you?

CHONEN'S VOICE

Yes.

LEAH

I remember. You had delicate hair and sad eyes; pale, mild hands with long, slender fingers, and every night belonged

to you, and every day you haunted me . . .
(*Little pause*)
Why did you leave me again?

CHONEN'S VOICE
Every wall they placed between us I knocked down, I
conquered death, but they were too many, and too strong;
and when they'd trampled out my flame in you, I left your
body so that I might come to your soul.

LEAH
Come to me my bridegroom, enter my heart, let me bear
you there, my dead man, till in dreams at night I can deliver
you, in dreams at night we can cradle the children we will
never have . . .

(*A wedding march is heard outside.*)

LEAH
They're bringing the stranger in, they want me to marry
him.
Come to me my bridegroom.

CHONEN'S VOICE
I left your body to return to your soul.

(*Wearing white for his wedding, Chonen appears.*)

LEAH
The circle's broken! I am coming to you! I'm so afraid!

CHONEN
Please, come to me.

LEAH
I am!

(As the wedding march grows stronger, Leah removes her black cloak and approaches the bridegroom. The two become one. The Messenger enters. Rabbi Azriel follows, the others behind him. Azriel stops them by the door.)

LEAH

(In a faraway voice) He is light and I am flame and we join into Holy fire and rise, and rise, and rise . . .

(Chonen lowers Leah's lifeless body to the floor. He takes a flame from her breast, and stands apart, in a golden light, unseen, waiting . . .
The others gather around Leah's body.)

RABBI AZRIEL

It is too late.

SENDER

Leah . . .

THE MESSENGER

Boruch dayan ho-emes.

(The Rabbi looks at the Messenger.)

RABBI AZRIEL

(Softly) It doesn't matter. Tell Him that. The more cause He gives to doubt Him. Tell Him that. The deeper delves faith. Though His love become only abrasion, derision, excoriation, tell Him, I cling. We cling. He made us, He can never shake us off. We will always find Him out. Promise Him that. We will always find Him, no matter how few there are, tell Him we will find Him. To deliver our complaint.

THE MESSENGER
I accept the commission.

RABBI AZRIEL
Sender, tip the messenger.

SENDER
My daughter.

(Sender gives the Messenger a gold coin.)

RABBI AZRIEL
Travel swiftly.

THE MESSENGER
Blessed be the true judge. May they rest in Paradise.

(The lights die. Leah rises and joins Chonen in his golden light; they dance until darkness overwhelms the stage. In darkness we hear the lone voice again:)

A LONE VOICE, CHANTING
Why did the soul,
Oh tell me this,
Tumble from Heaven
To the Great Abyss?
The most profound descents contain
Ascensions to the heights again . . .

END OF PLAY

CPSIA information can be obtained
at www.ICGtesting.com
Printed in the USA
LVHW041601090119
603305LV00021B/1246/P

9 780881 457056